Discover! America's
Great River Road
Volume 2
Illinois, Iowa, Missouri

The Middle Mississippi

by
Pat Middleton

Heritage Press · WI
Route 1, Stoddard, WI 54658

Pat Middleton is also the author of *Discover! America's Great River Road, Volume 1 (WI, MN, IA).* ©1988, 1989, and 1991. 224 pages. Heritage Press/WI. paper, $9.95, ISBN 09620823-0-9 and ISBN 0-9620823-3-3 (Third revision).

Copyright © 1992 by Pat Middleton

Published by Heritage Press · WI
Stoddard, WI 54658
608-457-2734

ISBN 0-9620823-1-7
Library of Congress Catalogue Card Number: 88-2228
First Edition, Volume 2

*-- Dedicated to my parents,
who taught me to follow my dreams;
and to Black Hawk, who fought for his.*

Contents

PREFACE

In choosing to explore the Middle Mississippi, one truly ventures into the soul of America. While the story here is inextricably bound to the story of the Upper Mississippi-- peopled by fur traders, immigrant farmers and laborers, busi- nessmen, and native Americans--it is the dramatic scope of its history which bestows national importance onto the Middle Mississippi.

This Middle Mississippi was a grand arena for most of the 18th and 19th centuries. Throughout the route, the legendary spirits of Marquette and Jolliet, Robert E. Lee, Thomas Jefferson, Lewis and Clark, Abe Lincoln, Mark Twain, and Brigham Young, ride with the traveler like holograms in a Disney amusement park.

Here was the focus of adventuring, social experimenta- tion, entrepreneurial and political expansion, and the pursuit of personal freedoms--freedom to live and worship in peace, freedom from the specter of human slavery.

But one man's freedom too often infringes upon that of another; and the poignant battle between the new settlers and the American natives rings loudly through the Mississippi River valley. *Black Hawk, Keokuk,* and *The Prophet* are names that bear respect in the Midwest. These were people with an abiding love for their homeland. Black Hawk's farewell still echos along the shoreline, *"I love the great river...Mine was a beautiful country. Now it is yours. Keep it as we did."*

It struck me, as I traveled, that these new immigrants proved worthy of their charge. Their settlements prosper. Their values endure. And their children love this river and the land.

Acknowledgements

It is somewhat daunting to begin acknowledgements knowing that most of those who helped can not be specifically thanked here. Please know that I carry those thanks in my heart.

In addition, I must thank each of the area Convention and Visitor Bureaus (CVBs). This book could not have been produced without their support, encouragement, and knowledgeable resources. All maps in this guide have been provided by area tourism bureaus or by the respective state departments of transportation.

Then to the many individual river buffs and historians who visited with me at length or gave permission to reproduce photos, sketches, paintings, and bits of previously published material; their efforts add immeasurably to our appreciation of the Middle Mississippi River valley. The cover photo by photographer Larry Knudson of Prairie du Chien, WI, captures what I believe is the "real" attraction of the river, its timeless heritage and grace.

My sincere thank you to friends and associates who carefully read or edited manuscripts: Dorothy Overson, Bernette Hummel, Margaret Larson, and Robert Fisher. Also, many individuals have contacted me from around the nation to comment on *Volume 1* of ***Discover! America's Great River Road***. In sharing your enthusiasm for the river and my first book, you provided the energy and focus which made this second volume a reality. *Thank you.*

Finally, there is a little family group which bears so gracefully the day-to-day clutter and distraction of an author-mom and spouse. To Lisa, Laura, and Rich, all my love!

--*Pat Middleton*

HOW TO USE THIS BOOK

The route followed by the maps and commentary in this guide commences in Dubuque, IA, near the junction of Illinois, Iowa, and Wisconsin. This tri-state area of deeply dissected valleys, ridges, and limestone outcroppings on both sides of the river is considered to be one of the more beautiful portions of the adjoining states. Therefore, the reader is guided first in a loop, south from Dubuque and Guttenberg, IA, to Galena and Savanna along the Illinois shore; then north again from Sabula to Dubuque, Iowa.

South of Savanna, IL, begins a broad agricultural flatland--the Mississippi River floodplain. The Mississippi River and the Great River Road meander back and forth across this great alluvial floodplain, touching first the eastern bluffs then the western bluffs and numerous cities, large and small. State parks, waysides, and national refuge amenities offer opportunities to visit remnant prairie patches, wilderness wetlands, and to enjoy boating, camping, fishing, or hiking.

From Hannibal, MO, (the boyhood home of American author, *Mark Twain)* through Alton, IL, and the *Cahokia Mounds World Heritage Site* just east of St. Louis, the rugged bluff country along either side of the river often resembles the Ozark Mountains of Arkansas. It is considered to be another more beautiful stretch of the river.

Historical and other background information is included in the *Table of Contents* under the heading of *Special Features*. I hope you will also enjoy several 'up close and personal' interviews labeled *Insight* which include reflections from various persons whose lives are closely intertwined with that of the river--a birder, a riverboat pilot, the "Clam Lady." *Volume 2* includes numerous brief histories and an *Index*.

The state and federally designated *Great River Road* is signed in green and white with the pilot's wheel symbol used throughout this book. Established in 1939 with the cooperation of ten states adjoining the Mississippi River, the Great River Road Parkway is a program of Federal *(herein designated as USH)*, State *(STH)*, and County *(CTH)* highway improvement along both sides of the Mississippi River, from Canada to the Gulf of Mexico. Federally funded scenic easements, roadside parks, scenic overlooks, off-road parks and forests, points of historical interest, and other public river-oriented facilities have been developed along both sides of the river.

This Guide also includes private amenities of interest to the traveler such as campgrounds, Bed & Breakfasts (herin referred to as *B&Bs)*, marinas, and seasonal/recreational attractions along the Mississippi River in Illinois, Iowa, and Missouri.

Volume 1, of *Discover! America's Great River Road,* begins at Prescott, WI, near St. Paul, MN, and follows the Great River Road to Dubuque, IA. Copies of *Volume 1* are available from most bookstores and many giftshops along the Mississippi River. See page 246 for order information.

The real beauty of the Great River Road lies in traveling slowly; stopping to absorb the view, chatting with locals at the cafe. It is our Rhine River, an Everglades of the north with a national treasure of eagles, wildlife, and migrating waterfowl. Here is America's heartland, where great moments in American and European history have played out for 300 years; where the passing of an elegant paddlewheeler endures as a grand event.

*It is my hope that this book will cause you to pause for a moment to enjoy an area bounded by, nurtured by, and challenged by a great river. For in the end--whether Indian, fur trader, adventurer, immigrant, visitor or farmer--we are **all** travelers.   Only the bluffs and the river are here to stay.*

--Pat Middleton

GUTTENBERG CIVIC CLUB

Ice-fishing shanties accumulate at various fishing "hot spots" along the Mississippi River. This shanty town is photographed out of Guttenberg, IA.

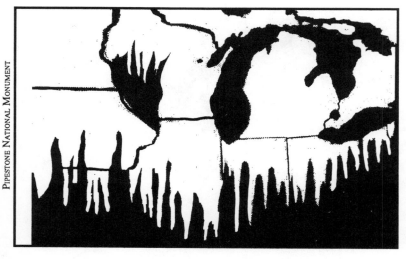

PIPESTONE NATIONAL MONUMENT

Glaciated flatlands (shown in white) of the Mississippi River Valley contrast sharply with unglaciated blufflands north of Dubuque/Galena and around Calhoun County, IL (just north of St. Louis).

GEOLOGY, GEOGRAPHY, AND NATURAL RESOURCES OF THE MIDDLE MISSISSIPPI RIVER VALLEY

For the traveler, the most noticeable geographic characteristic along the Great River Road from Dubuque to St. Louis will be the contrast between the unglaciated and glaciated portions of the Mississippi River valley.

The southern tip of a driftless or unglaciated peninsula dips down from the Minnesota/Wisconsin border to just south of Bellevue, IA. As the name Bellevue implies, this is considered by many to be the most beautiful portion of the upper river. Another scenic unglaciated section occurs just north of St. Louis, MO, between Hannibal, MO, and Alton, Illinois. Though surrounded time and again by glacial advances, these deeply dissected valleys, ridges, and bluffs were never actually encroached upon by the ice flows reshaping the rest of North America from 150,000 to 12,000 years ago.

The barren limestone bluffs of the river valley are mantled in a thick layer of *loess* (pronounced LESS), a rich, silt-like layer of clay and silt blown in by the wind from vast mud flats and river beds laid bare as glacial meltwaters receded.

The gently rolling farmland so characteristic of the rest of Illinois, Iowa, and Missouri, is the result of the grinding action and deposits of advancing and receding glaciers--rivers of ice often a mile deep which pulverized the earth beneath them. Glacial deposits of sand, clay, rocks, and gravel are referred to as *drift*. This soil and abundant minerals deposited by receding glaciers, meltwater, and wind, have blanketed the rolling Midwestern prairies to depths of 20 to 200 feet; the mother lode for the agricultural riches of the Midwest.

It was the leveling influence of the glaciers that made possible the vast grass prairies encountered by early settlers in Illinois. Prevailing dry, southwesterly winds fanned periodic wildfires that roared through vast acreages of flatland. While the deep-rooted grasslands not only survived but benefited from the cleansing fires, young trees were prevented from taking hold. Thus the old oak-hickory savannas are most commonly found in unglaciated areas where it was less likely that devouring wildfires would succeed at leaping deeply dissected valleys or that southwesterly winds could blow unimpeded.

Native sand, short-grass, and hill prairies along today's Great River Road have largely been destroyed by agriculture and the extinguishing of wildfires. Native fire resistant vegetation (such as little-bluestem, Side-oats Grama, and oak and hickory forests) have been replaced by invading dogwoods, rosebud, and sugar maples.

Bluffs along the Great River Road range in height from less than 100 feet to a high of 600 feet at Pinnacle Point in Clarksville, MO. Most rise about 200 feet above the broad alluviated flood plains or bottomlands and provide scenic lookouts over the vast river system and neighboring agricultural land.

Like the bluffs to the north, these are comprised mostly of shale, limestone, and sandstone--reefs and sediments laid down in warm, shallow oceans, 300 to 600 million years ago when central Illinois and the Appalachian Mountains lay directly under the equator. Bands of very hard limestone called *chert* provided Native Americans with a local substitute for flint.

Lime and cement factories are encountered throughout the valley, as are silica sand mines, and rock quarries. Such quarries provide an abundant flow of fossils, including ancient flora, land, and sea creatures.

The bluffs provided early settlers with an almost unlimited supply of limestone for construction of homes and commercial buildings. Many of these stone buildings dating from the 1840s through the 1890s still grace river towns. St. Donatus, IA, boasts the best collection of Luxembourger stone masonry in the new world.

Town names like Carbon Cliff and Coal Valley refer to coal mining which occured in many spots along the Illinois shore. As the continental plates began drifting northward, coal formed from thick plant layers which followed the retreat of the inland sea. With intense pressure and heat, a 15 foot layer of plant debris might yield a one-foot vein of coal.

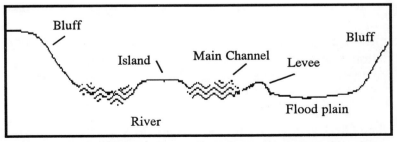

The profile of the Middle Mississippi often includes a broad floodplain protected from the main river channel by a raised levee.

Weather

The weather in the river valley is that of seasonal extremes. Quincy, IL, has a record high of 114 degrees Fahrenheit while northwestern Illinois has a record low of -35.

Thunder and lightning storms, as well as tornadoes, are increasingly common in this portion of the river valley as warm, humid air from the gulf collides with cooler air from Canada or the northwest. Severe weather warnings are announced on radio and TV. A *watch* indicates that conditions are right for a severe storm to develop. A *warning* indicates that there is immediate danger, and shelter should be sought.

For the most part, however, variable conditions prevail. During the winter, expect northwesterly winds. In summer, winds are mainly from the southwest and the traveler can expect lots of sunshine, cool nights, warm, and sometimes humid, days.

The River and Early Settlement

The compelling energy behind America's early 18th century interest in the Middle Mississippi was fueled by the lust for *western expansion*. The newly acquired *Louisiana Purchase* stretched from the Mississippi River to the Rocky Mountains. Together, the Missouri and the Mississippi river drained fully one third of the fledgling nation--and provided a ready transportation system for those determined to scout it out. Today, portions of thirty-one states are within that drainage area.

In 1804, President Thomas Jefferson dispatched William Clark and Meriwether Lewis up the Missouri River from St. Louis. Their accomplishments in following the Missouri to its source and then descending the Columbia River to the Pacific

Ocean are commemorated by the 630-foot high Gateway Arch at the Jefferson National Expansion Memorial in St. Louis. At the same time, Lt. Zebulon Pike struck north, up the Mississippi River. Many river towns are located near sites suggested by Pike for government forts. In fact, the *original* Pike's Peak is located at Pike's Peak State Park near McGregor, IA.

White traders and entrepreneurs opened up the Mississippi River wilderness by establishing trading posts near government forts and fur "factories." Millions of dollars in luxurious furs were shipped either north to Mackinac, MI, or south to St. Louis along the vast Mississippi waterway.

Black Hawk, a famous Sac warrior, led the battle to stem the white tide washing over the Indian cornfields along the Rock and the Mississippi rivers. After the Black Hawk Purchase in 1832, army veterans of the Black Hawk War carried east stories of this beautiful river valley and adjoining grassy plains. The tide of humanity became a tidal wave as immigrants and easterners raced to claim a stake in the prairie seas to the west.

Steamboats by the thousands soon roamed the Mississippi River loaded with passengers and supplies. In the 1840s came merchants and politicians, many of them German. A second wave, in the 1860s, brought great communities of Europeans: farmers and laborers from Ireland, Scandinavia, and Germany.

In the late 1850s and 1860s, railroads stretched west across the Mississippi River transforming river towns into bustling wholesale distribution centers for pioneers who pushed on to settle the plains states or to forge trails to California, Utah, and Oregon. Rock Island, IL, Muscatine, Davenport, and Clinton, IA, and Hannibal, MO, became portals to the west, providing lumber, floated in huge log rafts from Wisconsin and Minnesota, for houses across the treeless prairies.

During the Civil War, the Mississippi River offered the Union Army troops convenient transportation to the south. Confederate POWs were transported north to prison camps at Alton, IL, and Arsenal Island near Davenport or to hospitals and cemeteries on Arsenal Island and at Keokuk, IA. The victorious Union General, Ulysses S. Grant, rounded up his first volunteer command from Galena, IL. Abraham Lincoln was a respected western lawyer before he became a celebrated president.

As the frontier, the railroads, and the population centers pushed westward, many of these robust river towns lost their important economic and political influence. Populations today are sometimes much less than they were during the 1880s. Yet, all thrive with agriculture, manufacturing, finance and tourism playing significant economic roles. A preponderance of nationally known companies still have headquarters along the river-- Trane, John Deere, HON, Anheuser Busch--a tribute to the tenacity of early merchants and to the strategic location of Mississippi River towns.

Guttenberg, IA, to Dubuque, IA

DUBUQUE COUNTY

Dubuque and Guttenberg, Iowa

City of Dubuque, Iowa
Population 57,546

All roads lead to Dubuque. And no matter which highway brings one into town, the exit for the *Port of Dubuque Iowa Welcome Center* and the *Ice Harbor* will be well marked. Shuttles scurry from hotels to the Ice Harbor depositing visitors at the doorstep of Iowa's first *riverboat casino* and its newest and largest Welcome Center.

Located in the newly renovated warehouse of the old *Diamond Jo Steamboat Line,* the welcome center offers Iowa tourism information and an Iowa products gift shop. The ticket offices and gift shops of the *Dubuque Casino Belle* are located in the grand lobby on the harbor side of the building. The Ice Harbor is the home port for the *Casino Belle* which offers casino gambling year round.

The National Rivers Hall of Fame is located on the 2nd floor of the welcome center, the *Dubuque Heritage Museum* on the 3rd. The fourth floor observation area offers views of the city and the river.

Long lines of traffic are now a fact of life. Only the adventurous take a jaunt to Dubuque without reservations for lodging. Dubuque, the first Iowa city to embrace Greyhound racing, was also the first to license a riverboat casino. Therein lies the key to the economic revival of this once quiet river city.

What to See in Dubuque (Keyed to City map below)

THE ICE HARBOR *(23)* was built by the Army Corps of Engineers in the mid-1880s to shelter boats over-wintering in Dubuque. The Harbor hums with the coming and going of tour busses, and the colorful paddlewheelers of *Roberts River Rides* churn eagerly at the dock. *The Dubuque Casino Belle,* at 389 feet long and 53 feet high, dwarfs the excursion paddlewheelers.

THE WOODWARD RIVERBOAT MUSEUM *(28)* is one of the finest historical museums along the river and offers an extensive collection of regional books. Three dimensional, hands-on displays bring to life the diverse elements that have formed the fabric of life along the Mississippi during the past 300 years: Indians, fur traders, lead mining, steamboats, logging, clamming, and the natural scenic beauty of the Mississippi River gorge.

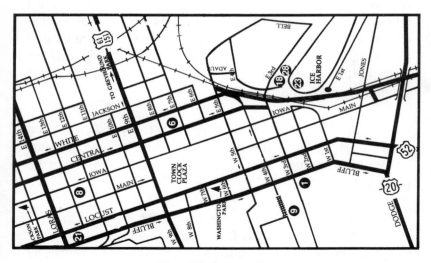

City of Dubuque, Iowa

ST. LUKE'S METHODIST CHURCH (12th and Main) boasts over 110 *Tiffany stained glass windows.* A sole non-Tiffany window, seen upon entering the sanctuary, provides a clear contrast to the Tiffany windows throughout the building.

FENELON SQUARE ELEVATOR *(9)* or TRAMWAY climbs 189 feet to the top of a 300 foot bluff overlooking the Ice Harbor. Built in 1882 by a local banker who desired to speed his trip home to the top of the bluff, the inclined railway is one of only three such cable cars in the area.

Fenelon Place was one of the most prestigious residential areas of Dubuque in the mid-19th century. Bankers, architects, lead and logging magnates built the prominent sturdy *Georgian Revival* style mansions such as those seen at 710 and 732 Fenelon. Several guides to Dubuque's historic architecture are available at the Riverboat Museum.

CABLE CAR SQUARE AND SHOPS *(9)* at the foot of the tramway and HARBOR PLACE MALL at the Ice Harbor offer fine arts, crafts, pottery, stained glass, antiques, china, and clothing.

THE OLD SHOT TOWER *(22)* is visible from the tramway summit. Built in 1856, it produced lead shot during the Civil War. The neighboring Zele Brewery opens its taste-testing rooms from 11 a.m. to 6 p.m.

DUBUQUE MUSEUM OF ART/OLD JAIL AND COUNTY COURTHOUSE *(6)*.The stately golden-domed County Courthouse was built in 1893. The neighboring jail is built in a rare *Egyptian Revival* style. Both structures are on the National Register of Historic Places. The art museum is closed Mondays.

THE GREYHOUND RACING TRACK is well signed. Be aware of numerous one-way streets. Follow 9th street out onto the island where the Greyhound Park and the Dubuque Yacht Basin are located.

Campers will enjoy *Riverview Park and Campground* which is directly beyond the Greyhound racing park and left along the riverfront. It is right on the river with no railroad tracks in earshot. **No swimming,** please, as the undertow is dangerous. Site of the Dubuque *International Dragon Boat* races. Picnic tables · grills · electricity · water

EAGLE POINT PARK (164 acres located on west Shiras Avenue). A beautiful park with scenic overlooks of the river and Lock & Dam #11. Picnic tables·playgrounds·stone shelters · tennis courts

The Tollbridge Restaurant, directly below Eagle Point Park at the west end of Rhomberg Avenue, offers diners a comfortable perch for winter eagle watching!

THE HERITAGE BIKING TRAIL runs between Dubuque and Dyersville, IA, and offers seasonal opportunities for hiking, biking, skiing, snowmobiling, and nature study on a converted railbed. The 26 mile long trail is fairly level and accented by rock outcroppings and meandering streams.

THE MINES OF SPAIN/LYONS INTERPRETIVE CENTER is located about 1/2 mile past the large furniture store at the intersection of *USH 52* and *USH 20*. Well worth a visit. There are fossils, a live rattlesnake, an eagle's nest, and historical and natural history information on display. Indian mounds and lead diggings are visible along the nature trails. The *Julien Dubuque Monument* is located on the property.

SPECIAL EVENTS

DubuqueFest, 3rd weekend in May. All-Arts Festival. Juried arts and crafts fair, dance, drama, house tours, ethnic food, and more.

The Great Mississippi Sailboat Race, mid-June. The race from Bellevue, IA, to Dubuque is the longest sailboat race on the Mississippi River.

Mathias Ham House Ice Cream Social, July 4th. Lincoln Ave., Dubuque. Food, beverages, and historic interpretation.

Craft Fair at Washington Park, first Sunday in August. 6th and Locust Streets, Dubuque.

Riverfest, September. Dubuque Ice Harbor. Focus on river history; activities, parade, arts, crafts, Venetian Parade.

A Brief History of Dubuque

The history of Dubuque, like that of Galena, IL, is intimately intertwined with the rest of the old Wisconsin Territory. In fact, both Dubuque and Galena (as well as Chicago) were added to the Illinois territory only after it became questionable whether there were enough votes to make Illinois a free (non-slave) state.

Julien Dubuque secured a claim to the lead rich area of present-day Dubuque from the Spanish in 1790, long before the Galena lead rush peaked in 1830. Julien, who originally worked the area as a fur trader, eventually developed the *Spanish Lead Mines* with his Indian wife.

Julien Dubuque died before the steamboat was invented, however, so he was never able to ship out highly profitable quantities of the mineral. After his death, the area came under complete Indian control. There was no further lead mining until the late 1820s after the *Virginia* became the first steamboat to travel north to Fort Snelling. By 1833, present-day Iowa was opened to settlement. In 1837 the Territorial Government of Wisconsin permitted the village of Dubuque to incorporate.

As the prosperity of the lead mines declined, agriculture began to flourish. Flour and grist mills, the railways and lumbering industries each made their mark on the county.

During the mid-19th century, excursions into the scenic upper Mississippi provided an important source of riverboat income. Tourists as well as settlers were flocking up-river. A journal entry from 1830 notes:

Tourists swarm to the Mississippi River, as well as immigrants. Here are thrown together people of every country and every character. You may see one day English, Irish, German, French, Swiss, Indian, fur trader and Americans, and in such a variety of national customs and costumes as is rarely to be found, in any other place.

The Diamond Jo steamboat line, founded in Dubuque by "Diamond Joe" Reynolds in 1862, eventually became one of the largest packet companies on the Mississippi River carrying freight and passengers.

In 1857, the City of Dubuque recorded one thousand steamboat landings. After the 1850s, the railroads started to ply the river banks and soon snatched the bulk of the freight and passenger service from the steamboats.

CAMPGROUNDS IN THE DUBUQUE/GALENA AREA

Dubuque Yacht Basin RV Park -- 16th Street and the River. Across from the Greyhound Park. Electricity, showers, swimming pool, laundry, convenience store, game room. Shuttle to Dog Park.

Mud Lake Marina -- 6 miles north of Dubuque. Fishing, camping, electricity.

Palace Campground -- 1 mile west of Galena on *USH 20*. Camping, swimming pool, full hook-ups and showers.

Riverview Park Campgrounds -- Off Kerper Blvd. in Dubuque. Just beyond the Greyhound Park and left along the river. Some electricity. Directly on the river, no railroad nearby. Boating, playground, fishing.

Rustic Barn Campground -- 3854 Dry Hollow Road, Kieler, WI, just off *USH 61-151* south of Dickeyville, WI.

Guttenberg, Iowa
Population 2,257

Perhaps this Clayton County town, 40 miles north of Dubuque on *USH 52*, should have appeared in Volume 1 of ***Discover! America's Great River Road.*** As it is, it proves the adage that Midwesterners have a tendency to keep their favorite places to themselves. Meandering bluffside drives provide memorable river overlooks. The Mississippi Valley Overlook just south of town is easily missed, but the visitor is rewarded with a sweeping upriver view. And unless you race past on *USH 52*, completely missing the historic riverfront "old town," Guttenberg will become a favorite of yours as well.

Limited edition print of Gutenberg by N.D. Shahrivan

The street names Hayden, Koerner, Mozart, and Goethe reflect the German heritage of the town, though it was originally settled by the French who called it "Prairie La Porte," or "Door to the Prairie." A story persists that when the predominantly German population voted to change the name to honor Johann Gutenberg, a disgruntled clerk (of French extraction) misspelled the name so that the town became, forever, Guttenberg (with a double 't').

Johann Gutenberg is credited with inventing the first printing press with moveable type. His Bible was printed in Mainz, Germany, in 1436 or 1437. A facsimile of that first Bible is displayed at the Guttenberg Public Library on Second Street, kitty-korner from the double spires of St. Mary's Church.

Guttenberg's "old town" is listed in the National Historic Register and is located just down river of the mile-long levee of *Riverview Park* and *Lock & Dam 10*. Plan to park the car anywhere along River Park Drive and enjoy a leisurely rivertown stroll. Part of the scenic nature of the old town lies in its old stone buildings, and the good chance that even a casual walker can spot a 100-year old clamshell (filled with holes where button blanks were sawed out) in the grass.

LOCK & DAM 10, near the Aquarium. Observation platform ·restrooms. Eagle-watching can be excellent in the open water on colder days from November to March.

UPPER MISSISSIPPI RIVER FISHERIES MANAGEMENT STATION AND AQUARIUM offers a rare opportunity to see live native fishes and reptiles: bass, pike, river sturgeon, several varieties of turtles, and even a gar fish. Notice that there are several soft-shelled turtles that inhabit backwaters of the Mississippi River.

There is also an informative display of fresh water mussels with such curious names as *Warty Back, Pig's Eye, Pocketbook,* and *Washboard.* The pearl buttons used before the turn of the century were produced from Mississippi River mussels (popularly called clams) along the entire length of the Upper Mississippi River. Children will enjoy visiting the aquarium. Open 8 a.m. to 4:30 p.m., May through September.

DIAMOND JO WAREHOUSE RESTAURANT is another well-disguised "favorite." It is housed in an old stone warehouse built in 1856 by the Galena, IL, family of Ulysses S. Grant for the purchase and storage of hides. Between 1864 and 1891 the Diamond Jo Reynolds steamboat line used it as a warehouse. This restaurant is so river-oriented that they've neglected to post much of a sign on the street side of the building. But the food and the prices are good, and the river view is excellent. A comfortable spot for winter eagle watching. If at first you don't find it, *ask.*

An interesting photo history of the Diamond Jo line is displayed in the restaurant. The *Diamond Lady* Casino in Bettendorf, IA, is modeled after one of the Diamond Jo excursion boats. In Dubuque, the Iowa Welcome Center is located in another restored warehouse of the Diamond Jo line.

KANN IMPORTS is truly an anomoly. Little would one expect to find a marketplace for exquisite French lead crystal, handmade porcelains, or copper and bronze sculptures from around the world in such a quiet country town.

"Oh, people find us," Carl Kann tells me assuredly as *we trade yarns on the bench in front of the shop. "We've always just sought out those items we find most beautiful. People hear about us, and for over 50 years they've come--from all over the United States and from many, many foreign countries."*

INSIGHT

Marian Havlik
"The Clam Lady"

"Technically, freshwater mussels (commonly called clams) should be found everywhere along the upper Mississippi River, but they're almost non-existent except north of Keokuk, IA, where there is still suitable habitat. South of the Missouri River there is just too much silt. Mussels are usually found in narrow bands along the main channel and throughout the major backwaters. Illinois recently named six or seven of these breeding areas as mussel sanctuaries.

"Because mussels are filter feeders, their absence or presence provides an early environmental monitor--like canaries that miners used to take with them into the mines. If a stretch of river has clams in it, you know it is suitable for fish, and humans, as well. It's all interrelated.

"One of our biggest environmental scares occurred during the mussel die-off between 1982 and 1985. For 400 miles from La Crosse south, mussels of all species seemed to be dying a sudden death that caused the meats to separate from the shells. A toxin may have been involved. As many as 40-50% of the Washboard and Three-Ridges may have died. A scientific study done one day in Pool 10 indicated that 38,000 mussels had died recently. Unrelated studies also show fish die-offs during the same period.

"What actually happened--whether it was a chemical spill, a natural toxic algae bloom, a widely used herbicide or pesticide, or a combination of these which caused the problem--was never determined. Hindsight indicated that the end of the die-off coincided with the banning of the chemical ALAR in the apple orchards along the river, but ALAR may not have been the answer.

"The demand for mussel shells from the Japanese cultured pearl industry has greatly increased since 1980. Nationally, 5,000 to 6,000 tons of shells go to Japan every year. Probably half of that amount is from the Mississippi River. Depending on the state, mussels which might be harvested include the Three-Ridge, Washboard, Pig Toe, Pimple Back, Heel-Splitter, and Mapleleaf.

"Most states have begun to realize that while mussels are a harvestable resource, they are also a limited resource. The pearl button industry at the turn of the century ended when there were just not enough clams to harvest anymore. Most Midwestern states now regulate the clamming season. Clammers don't always like that, but just as with deer, fish, and other harvestable species, the clams must be protected.

"In mid-June, 1991, the introduced Zebra Mussel was documented 50 miles from the mouth of the Illinois River in Pearl, Illinois. By mid-September researchers found the Zebra Mussel 500 miles north, near my home in La Crosse, WI.

"Zebra Mussels will change the Mississippi River, the native mussel fauna, and perhaps the fish fauna, as we now know it! The Zebra Mussel was imported into the Great Lakes from northern Europe in the mid-1980s, apparently in the ballast waters of freighters. By 1990, it was found in the tributary rivers of lower Lake Michigan. From there, barges spread it to the Mississippi River.

"The problem with Zebra Mussels is the same as with other introduced species--they are prolific because they do not have any natural enemies. Even worse, this mussel glues itself to any hard surface such as native mussels, boat hulls, buoys, and water intake pipes. Native mussels or crayfish can be covered with hundreds of Zebra Mussels until their ability to move or simply to filter-feed is so inhibited that they die.

"The Zebra Mussel has already cost millions of dollars in the Great Lakes region because of clogging intake pipes of power plants and municipal water supplies. It won't be safe to leave your fishing boat motor in the water, for fear of clogging that water intake, too. Hopefully some controls can be found, and quickly."

MARIAN HAVLIK

Worse than any plague! Colonies of tiny Zebra Mussels glue themselves to the exposed shell of native mussels--or any other hard surface.

THE CASSVILLE (WI) FERRY leaves from the Turkey River Landing just south of Guttenberg on a 1/2 hour schedule between 9 a.m. and 9 p.m., weather permitting. The ferry carries 12 cars and offers an excellent opportunity to take a little river jaunt and explore the Wisconsin shore. Small fee.

Chapter 3 continues in Galena, IL. See Chapter 5 for the guide to the scenic drive on Iowa's Great River Road between Sabula and Dubuque.

Dubuque, and Jackson County, IA. Galena, and Savanna, IL,

JO DAVIESS COUNTY

Galena, Illinois

TOUR ROUTE: DUBUQUE, IA, TO GALENA, IL
15 miles to Galena on *USH 20, East*

Galena, Illinois
Population 3,800

The familiar Pilot's Wheel of *America's Great River Road* greets the traveler again on *USH 20* east out of Dubuque and toward Galena, IL. The road heads inland from East Dubuque, IL, into the rolling, agriculture-rich hills of Jo Daviess County. Just north of Galena, one begins to notice the flavor of southern cultural traditions fostered by Galena's close ties with the Mississippi River and communities down river. The colorful county name commemorates a Kentucky hero of the Civil War. The name was chosen, despite the wishes of the local constituency, by the overwhelming majority in the state house who had Kentucky roots.

These southern symphathies almost put Illinois on the side of the south during the Civil War. It was not until the coming of the railroads and the influx of Yankee farmers and businessmen that loyalties became widely focused on the northeast.

A Brief History of Galena

Galena's glory days came early and faded quickly with all the intensity of California's gold rush days. It was known since the 1680s that great deposits of lead were mined by the Indians to trade for European goods, but it was not until 1819 that 100 men came to establish a permanent commercial mining effort in what was then known as the Fever River.

In 1823, the *Virginia,* the first army steamboat to reach Fort Snelling in St. Paul, docked at the camp. It was the steamboat that made all the difference to Galena. Lead could now be shipped out in great (and heavy) quantity. In 1825 there may have been 200 people in the area--by 1828 there were somewhere between 5,000 and 10,000 hardy souls. The commercial district prospered as farmers and miners ventured out from Galena, returning for supplies and to ship out produce. The boom days were on!

The Civil War ripped through the country in 1861 and by 1865 Galena had its last burst of national reknown. In an ironic twist of fate, eight Union generals came from Galena. One of them, Ulysses S. Grant, rose to command the Union Army and accept the surrender of Gen. Robert E. Lee. In 1868, Grant became the 18th President of the United States.

By 1870, Galena's lead production was no longer nationally significant. Much of the population had followed the Gold Rush west or filtered north into Wisconsin, Iowa and Minnesota. The railroads by-passed this steamboat port, laying track directly from Chicago to Prairie du Chien and La Crosse,WI. As steamboat traffic faded, the Galena River sediment began silting in the Galena River so that today it (like the town it served) is only a pretty shadow of its former self.

What to See in Galena

Modern Galena is an architectural pastry shop. The commercial district built to serve the needs of 10,000 people 100 years ago remains almost completely intact. There has been little need for today's much smaller population to construct anything new.

The two major streets, Main and Bench (which is terraced up the hill above Main), are lined with commercial and public buildings dating from as early as the 1830s. Private homes, built to reflect the great wealth generated during the lead mining days, dot the hills throughout the village.

Galena's beautiful Victorian homes date mainly from the 1850s to the 1870s. In comparison, the historic homes in most towns up river will date from the 1880s to the 1900s. The *Ryan House*, *The Belvidere House*, and *Stillman's Country Inn* are just samples of the many elegant mansions built during the mid-19th century boom days.

The Ryan House greets visitors approaching Galena from the north.

Guided tours are available in several of the homes, including Grant's. Many others are open to the public as guest homes and Bed and Breakfast Inns. A complete list of lodging (including prices) is available from the *Visitor's Center, 101 Bouthillier St., Galena, IL   61036*. A printed *architectural walking tour* of the village is also available free from the center. The *Spring and Fall Home Tours* are among the most popular annual events in town.

Plan to treat yourself well during your stop in Galena. More than 25 antique shops and seemingly endless specialty boutiques are located in this town which is a shopper's dream. The *Truffles Restaurant* at the newly restored *DeSoto House Hotel* offers fine dining in a quiet, sunlit interior courtyard.

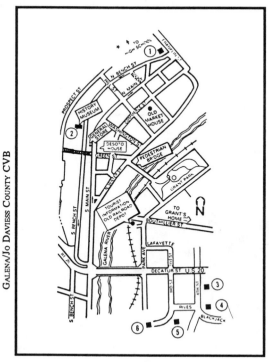

City of Galena Map

Pete's Steak House and *Clark's Restaurant* are local favorites for good home cooking. The ice cream shop promises home-made sugar cones, hot fudge, and old fashioned malts--all accompanied by a merry player piano.

Points of Interest

A first stop in Galena should be the *Visitor's Center* located in the old railroad depot on Bouthillier Street. Those arriving from the west on *USH 20* would cross the bridge over the Galena River and turn left. A large parking area is conveniently located to the Visitor Center, Grant Park, and the footbridge into historic Galena. Grant Park is a major city park on the bank of the Galena River offering picnicking, playground, and a picturesque view of the old town of Galena.

The *flood gates* guarding the commercial district protect the downtown area against flooding of the river as well as torrents of water which wash down *USH 20* during storms.

The OLD MARKET HOUSE on Commerce and Perry Streets is operated by the Illinois Historic Preservation Agency. The Main Hall has an *architectural exhibit* which helps the visitor recognize the many styles of Galena's buildings.

The COUNTY HISTORICAL MUSEUM is located at 211 South Bench Street. An excellent slide show on the history of Jo Daviess County is presented regularly through the day. Exhibits detail life during the lead mining and Civil War days. Nast's famous life size painting of Lee's Surrender to Gen. Grant fills one wall. Small fee.

The DESOTO HOUSE was built in 1855 for the grand price of $85,000. It had five stories, more than 200 rooms and was furnished with velvet carpets, rosewood furniture, satin curtains, intricately carved wood accents, marble table tops and statuary. Horace Greeley, James Russell Lowell, and Abraham Lincoln all stayed at the DeSoto. It formed the headquarters for Grant's presidential campaign. Today it has been elegantly restored and features several interesting shops which line the courtyard of the Truffles Restaurant.

GRACE EPISCOPAL CHURCH is located on Hill and Prospect Streets. It was built in 1847 to replace the frame chapel built in 1838. Its stained glass windows came from Belgium. Its organ, the first brought to the Northwest, was shipped to New Orleans from Philadelphia by sailing boat and then up the river on a steamboat.

PAT MIDDLETON

Galena seen from Grant Park

The FIRST PRESBYTERIAN CHURCH, built in 1838, is just down the block. According to Galena history, it was founded by a Yale and Princeton graduate who had appealed to the American Missionary Society for an assignment so difficult "that no one else will take it." During the 1840s, his was the largest church west of Chicago.

THE STOCKADE REFUGE is flanked by *Perry Street,* one of only three or four authentic cobblestone streets left in America. The stockade was built during the Black Hawk War at a time when fears of Indian uprisings could send many thousands of area farmers, miners and families fleeing to Galena for shelter. Indian artifacts are exhibited and some of the original stockade has been excavated. Small fee.

THE GALENA PIONEER CEMETERY is located on Washington Street, just behind *Grant's first home* at 121 High Street. The cemetery contains the graves of the area's earliest settlers and miners. Some graves date from before 1812 and contain remains brought west by people who made homes in Galena. Many of the miners from Cornwall are buried here. The land was donated by a Capt. Gear who came to the Galena lead diggings without a penny to his name. Eventually he discovered a lode on Tower Hill from which he took 26,000,000 pounds of ore. Lead ore at the time was selling for $80 a ton.

FOR A COMPLETE LODGING DIRECTORY OR FURTHER INFORMATION ON WHAT TO SEE OR DO CONTACT: The Galena/Jo Daviess County Convention and Visitors Bureau, 101 Bouthillier Street, Galena, IL. 61036 or call toll free (800) 747-9377. Call the Dubuque Convention and Visitors Bureau toll free at (800) 79-VISIT. Advance reservations are highly recommended in this area. For a list of campgrounds, please see page 17.

Upon leaving the city of Galena on USH 20 south, a progressively higher and more winding climb above the Galena River valley takes the traveler through a scenic, wilderness area of small coulees, steep ravines, and rocky outcroppings. The tremendous geologic forces which crushed the surrounding prairies lead to massive faulting and upheavels in this unglaciated island. Several recommended scenic rural drives to the east and north of Galena are described in brochures at the Galena visitor center.

CHESTNUT MOUNTAIN SKI AREA (Located on Blackjack Road). Year round vacation resort. Swim · ski · tennis · horse trails

TAPLEY WOODS WAYSIDE. Great views of the Apple River valley from both sides of the ridge top. Public hunting area.

LONG HOLLOW OVERLOOK (The exit for this outstanding scenic overlook is easily missed.) Tremendous views from the road, but if you find river bridges unnerving, you'll likely find your heart skipping a beat even from the parking lot. Three states are visible from the 60 foot high fire ranger lookout tower.

THE APPLE RIVER CANYON

According to the Illinois Department of Conservation, this dramatic canyon was formed by the winding waters of the Apple River. Immediately after the ice ages the canyon probably looked more like simple crevasse. The action of time and erosion gradually widened it into the vast valley or canyon seen today. Limestone bluffs, deep ravines, springs, streams and wildlife characterize this area which was once part of a vast seabottom that stretched from the Alleghanies to the Rocky Mountains. As the crushing, shearing weight of glaciers did not scar this driftless area, fossil remains of ancient sea creatures can still be found in surface limestone.

A state historical marker near the lookout describes a financial scheme developed by Scottish financier and adventurer, John Law. His *Company of the West* was formed in Paris in 1717, on the fraudulent claim that the Illinois lead mines were well-developed. In October of 1720 the royal bank of France merged with Law's company and, after wild speculation, both the scheme (dubbed the "Mississippi Bubble") and the royal bank of France collapsed, ruining its numerous investors.

While the "Mississippi Bubble" discredited the idea of a national bank in France, it did incite international interest in the colonization of the French Louisiana Territory.

In 1721 Phillip Francois de Renault came to the area with 200 miners and 500 Santo Domingan slaves. Only 20 miners were still on the Galena River in 1743.

> *3 miles to Elizabeth, IL. 40 miles to Freeport, IL. 19 miles to Savanna, IL. 30 miles to Dubuque, IA (north).*
>
> *Great River Road continues south on STH 84*

Elizabeth, Illinois
Population 750

Located just south of the Apple River valley on *USH 20,* its name aptly reflects the English and Irish roots of early settlers. Just for fun, make a stop at the historic *Busy Big Store* on Main Street. This is a classic old general store, with a moulded tin ceiling and everything from shoes to cheese and sausages. The parents of the proprietor, Erwin Bishop, came to the area as miners from Cornwall, England. His mother took up the mercantile business after the death of her husband.

Illinois' Great River Road, STH 84, is well inland of the Mississippi River until Mississippi Palisades State Park north of Savanna. It follows the bottomlands of the Apple River. Scenic drive continues south of Hanover, IL, where a gentle climb begins through ravines, dry washes.

SPECIAL EVENTS

Spring Tour of Homes and Skills from the Hills. Galena, early June. Traditional Arts and Crafts Displays.

Annual Galena Art Festival at the Old Market Historic Site. Mid-June. Juried Art Fair with more than 50 booths.

Old Fashioned 4th of July, Flea Market, and Antique Town Rod Run. 4th of July weekend.

Fall Tour of Homes. Galena, late September

Duck Fest, Hanover, IL. 1st weekend in October. Wildlife artists, flea market, decoy race, roast duck featured at the local cafe.

U.S. Grant Antique Market. Early Galena, October. Dealers from throughout the midwest gather under one roof.

Fall color tours, art/craft displays. Galena, 3rd weekend in October. Amtak trains make annual run from Chicago.

Hanover, Illinois
Population 1,100

Hanover is approximately opposite Lock & Dam 12 and Bellevue, IA. The town claims to be the *Mallard Duck Capital of the World* thanks to a local enterprise, *Whistling Wings,* which raises and sells millions of ducks worldwide to restaurants, game preserves, and "anyone who wants a mallard."

According to Marianne Whalen Murphy, daughter of founder Leo Whalen, the Whistling Wings ducklings have been sent as far away as Japan--to the ponds of Emperor Hirohito's palace. A presidential limousine once picked up mallards for Lyndon Johnson's Lone Star Ranch.

"We hatch and ship about 200,000 mallards annually," Marianne explained, "but most go to schools, zoos, and conservation groups."

Families will enjoy visiting the office and hatchery located in the center of town. Duck meat, pins, shirts, and even *guano* (duck manure) are available for sale to visitors.

DON WALSH

15,000 eggs spend 24 days in the incubator at the Whistling Wings hatchery. Above, thousands of day-old ducklings cuddle together in holding pens.

LIONS PARK is located just south of town as are the Whistling Wings rearing pens.

U.S. MILITARY RESERVATION and munitions depot begun in 1917 extends along the river bank between miles 545.2 and 558.5. Boaters are cautioned not to land along the Illinois shore in this area.

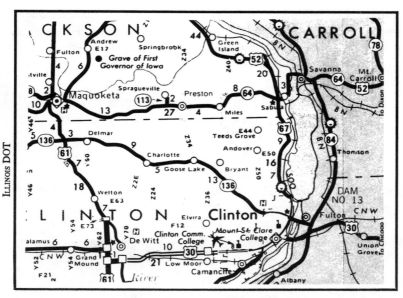

Savanna, IL, south to Clinton, IA.

Travelers may choose to cross the river at Savanna to Sabula, IA, and continue north in a loop back to Dubuque along Iowa's Great River Road. See Chapter 5, Jackson County.

CARROLL AND WHITESIDE
COUNTIES, ILLINOIS

Savanna, IL, to Clinton, IA

It was a prominent group of immigrants from the state of Maryland who named this county for Charles Carroll, a Marylander and signer of the Declaration of Independence. At his death in 1832 Carroll was 94 and the last surviving of the original signers. Another native of Carroll County, Nita Snook, was the flying instructor for Amelia Earhart.

Savanna, the first settlement south of Galena, was established at a crossroads of north-south and east-west trails used to access the lead mining region. The railroads followed many of these same early trails and, thereafter, many of the towns in Carroll County thrived or faded thanks to the presence or absence of a train depot.

LAKEWOOD RESORT (5 miles north of Savanna, on Mill Hollow Road just off *STH 84* north of Palisades Park). 142 acres, open year round. Hunting/fishing guide available. Camping · electric · swimming · fishing · picnicking · hiking

Almost without warning, the roadway which has followed the Apple River valley well inland is suddenly sandwiched between the Mississippi River and the ghostly white limestone

cliffs of the Mississippi Palisades State Park. A camping area is indicated north of the park's main entrance. This lovely portion of the northern route is the first stretch where the Mississippi River is actually in sight along the Illinois route.

MISSISSIPPI PALISADES STATE PARK (4 miles north of Savanna on *STH 84.)* Near the confluence of the Apple and Mississippi rivers. Named for steep limestone bluffs which border the Great River Road and the Mississippi River. Open year around. 2,500 acres. Scenic bluff area with grand river views, unusual hill prairies, and upland woods. Picnicking · hiking·camping·boat launch·fishing·winter sports·equestrian camp

USH 52 west crosses the Mississippi River just north of Savanna and follows an extensive causeway to *Sabula, IA.* This unique island city was salvaged by U.S. Army Corps of Engineers levees when the bottomland surrounding the town was flooded by the waters of Pool 13. It is well worth a side trip as there are many egrets, eagles, and other waterfowl inhabiting the wetland surrounding the town and causeways. (*SEE CHAP-TER 5, Jackson County, IA, to continue north on the Iowa shore through Bellevue, St. Donatus, and Dubuque. This chapter continues south along the Illinois shore, crossing the river at Fulton into Clinton, IA).*

FISHERMEN'S BEND FISH MARKET (located near the *USH 52* bridge on the Illinois shore) is now called *Flick's Fish.* Fresh, smoked, or live catfish are available along with bait, fishing licenses, and the latest local "fish stories."

Dixon, IL, (about 50 miles east on *USH 52)* is the hometown of former U.S. president, Ronald Reagan. Reagan was born in Tampico, IL, and attended school in Dixon. The Dixon home is restored and open to the public.

A life-size model of oxen pulling a Conestoga wagon at a roadside gift shop just north of Savanna on *STH 84,* is a first reminder, too, that Illinois really is the "Prairie State" as well as the end of the driftless corner of Wisconsin, Illinois, and Iowa. Here, flat, glaciated topography allowed overland travel (less expensive than passage on a steamboat) right to the river.

Savanna, Illinois
Population 4,529

By the 1890s, increasing shipments from western meat packing houses made Savanna a major junction for railroads to Rock Island and Sabula. Savanna once had 18 tracks and a round house. The Chicago, Milwaukee and St. Paul railroad ran east and west, the Burlington ran north and south. The commercial district and the extensive train switching area of this railroad transport center are arrayed in the lowlands along the river.

Distinguished Victorian mansions (some with widow's walks for river watching) sit on *Spinings Hill,* well above the workaday world--and the predictable floods of the Mississippi River. Only the most daring will try driving up the steep inclines of this "Quality Row." The most notable house is Havencrest on the *second* bluff high above Savanna. Built in 1899 by Simon Greenleaf it is five stories high with a tower which provides the most commanding view of the Mississippi River.

MILWAUKEE ROAD PASSENGER CAR and CABOOSE (downtown Savanna on the corner of Chicago Avenue and Main Street). The Chamber of Commerce office is located inside the passenger car--one of only 18 restored in the U.S. The caboose is located nearby.

MARQUETTE PARK (downtown Savanna on Wayne King Drive). Scenic park on the Mississippi. Picnicking·boat launch

OLD MILL PARK (East edge of Savanna on *USH 52).* Picnicking · playground · tennis courts · ball diamonds

47 miles to East Moline, IL. 8 miles to Thomson, IL.

A small town every eight miles seems to be a predictable pattern along the Mississippi River. It may have been because riverboats needed frequent refueling and inns and villages gradually sprang up around the woodcutter's cabin. Water towers for the trains were also spaced every 8 to 10 miles. Another possibility is that eight miles was a convenient one hour ride for a man on horseback. Because horses tire, a twenty mile distance would have been too lengthy a round trip for one day.

SPECIAL EVENTS

Melon Days, Labor Day Weekend in Thomson, IL. Free watermelons
Car Cruise and Beach Party, 3rd weekend in August at Savanna, IL, Old Mill Park.
Duck Fest, 1st weekend in October at Hanover, IL. Wildlife artists, flea market, decoy race, roast duck featured at local cafe.

BIG SLOUGH FEDERAL RECREATION AREA (4 miles north of Thomson, IL, on *STH 84.* Turn west on improved county road at the sign. Area is located 1/4 mile downstream of the *Fin and Feather Resort*). Water · boat launch · picnicking

SPRING LAKE (4 miles outh of Savanna on *STH 84).* On the Mississippi River. Good fishing year around, but draws hundreds of ice fishermen each winter. Boat launch · boat rentals · store · dump station

UPPER MISSISSIPPI RIVER WILDLIFE AND FISH REF-
UGE. Few visitors are aware that much of the Mississippi River
shoreline from Wabasha, MN, through St. Louis is federal fish
and wildlife refuge. *The Upper Mississippi River Wildlife and
Fish Refuge* extends for 260 miles from Wabasha to Rock
Island, IL.

Established in 1924, the refuge now includes over 200,000
acres under the joint protection of various state agencies, the
Fish and Wildlife Service, and the U.S. Army Corps of
Engineers. It serves primarily to provide sanctuary to waterfowl
migrating along the *Mississippi River Flyway.*

In addition to bald eagles, hawks, Canadian geese, and
Tundra swans, as much as 75% of the continental Canvasback
duck population may be seen during migration on the river. 270
species of birds, 57 types of mammals, 45 different amphibians
and reptiles, and 113 fish species have been identified within the
refuge. Boat launches, camping and picnic areas are maintained
throughout the refuge.

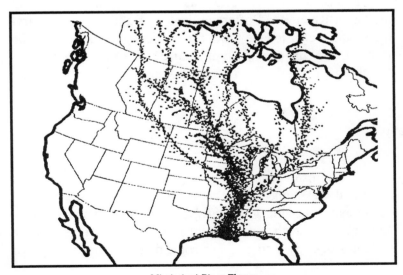

Mississippi River Flyway

SPRING LAKE WATERFOWL OVERLOOK. A small sign directs the visitor across unguarded tracks to a small parking area overlooking wetlands of Spring Lake.

A broad sand prairie *(Savanna* refers to a tree-dotted, grassy plain) opens up between Savanna and Thomson. Melons have been an important economic factor in the area since 1905 when a transplanted Wisconsin dairy farmer found that the barren sand produced more watermelon than milk. During the 1920s and 30s, twenty railroad cars a day were filled with melons to be shipped to Chicago. Wagon loads full of melons sold for less than $3. Today, the melon crop continues to require backbreaking hand hoeing, weeding, and picking.

Another new crop, potatoes, has recently been introduced by farmers from the potato-rich Golden Sands region of central Wisconsin. As the sand turns to a dark rich loam below Thomson, crops include corn, peas, and other vegetables. *Road markets in season.*

BUCK'S BARN RESORT. Restaurant in a restored barn along the Great River Road offers a display of antique agricultural tools, and a classic Chevrolet car collection. Children will be fascinated by the champion miniature horses bred on the site. No charge to view collections or horses. Motel · golf course

Thomson, Illinois
Population 700

Thomson developed along the Racine Railroad line in 1864 and was named for a company executive. The original settlement in the area was *Bluffville,* located about one mile east and one mile north, near natural fresh water springs and the Galena-Rock River stage coach route that ran along the foot of the bluffs. In the 1840s and 50s, the little settlement included a grist mill, post office, school, wagon shop, blacksmith, and saw mill.

The occupants and businesses gradually shifted to Thomson and the railroad depot. There is now only a unique *grout house* and a brick house to mark the original site of Bluffville. Grout houses are constructed of ground limestone, river shells, straw, and other materials, all tamped into molds which are elevated until the house is the desired height. The exterior is finished with stucco. It is a style of construction seen more often along the border of Luxembourg in Europe.

Today, Thomson promotes itself as the melon (and sandburr) capital of the world. The Watermelon Cafe is located next to the McGinnis Melon Market on *STH 84* and offers home cooking from locally grown squash, sweet corn, and other vegetables. In season, try a watermelon malt!

THOMSON RAILROAD DEPOT MUSEUM is open May through October and contains railroading memorabilia. The depot is typical of those built in small towns. Free. Public playground and restrooms nearby.

THOMSON CAUSEWAY (At the end of Main Street, adjacent to the west edge of Thomson on the Mississippi River). This largest public use area on the Mississippi River is a Class A Army Corps of Engineers recreational facility. Camping · electricity·dump station·boat launch·fishing·picnicking·hiking ·park rangers

WHITESIDE COUNTY, ILLINOIS

This county is named for Gen. Samuel Whiteside, who, in the early 1800s, led a force of volunteers up the Rock River just southeast of Fulton and burned the Winnebago village of *White Cloud* (the Prophet) near the current site of Prophetstown, IL. Nearby is *Prophetstown State Park* and *Tampico,* the birthplace of former U.S. president, Ronald Reagan. A self-guided historical tour of the county is available; contact Whiteside County (see *Tourism Contacts,* appendix).

LOCK AND DAM 13 (Two miles north of Fulton, on *STH 84.* Turn west at the sign.) Built in 1939 at a cost of $7,643,000. Pool 13 (above the dam) is the widest pool along the upper Illinois shore. Four miles wide at a point 2.5 miles north of the dam. Observation area · boat launch · picnic area

This, like each of the 27 locks along the river, is an excellent spot to watch for wintering eagles. The water is open throughout the winter, and fish injured while going through the dam make easy hunting for the big birds.

SCHAEFFER'S FISHERY at the intersection for the Lock and Dam, offers fresh and smoked fish. River catfish are still shipped to Chicago in "live tanks" although farm raised "cats" from the south have devastated the market for river fish.

Fish markets are interesting places to visit along the river. The fishermen haul in washtubs and wooden boxes full of carp, buffalo, catfish and bullheads about mid-morning. Once the main rush is over, the market owner is often quite happy to provide a tour of the processing room, live tank, and his collection of various river oddities that have come up on his lines through the years. Be prepared, though, for wet floors and the over-powering smells of river and fish. Schaeffer's is also a shell camp, purchasing mussel shells from professional divers (See page 121).

Fulton, Illinois
Population 4,000

While the Dutch were not the original settlers of this low-lying area of the river, it was the Dutch who were prominent after 1856. Once known as *Dutchtown* or *Hollandtown,* in 1855 the city was named for Robert Fulton, one of the inventors of the steamboat.

Families named Akker, Dykema, Vandellan, Sikkema, and Nannanga braved ocean voyages lasting as long as 75 days. They knew how to drain, dike, and farm the soggy bottoms in the area, and, by the 1890s, the Dutch Reformed Church built in 1869 had over 1,000 people in the congregation.

Many families continue to pass on fearsome tales of the trials immigrants experienced with early ocean travel. A rough-hewn wooden fork commemorates seven days spent floating at sea after the ship goes down in a storm. The prosperous descendents of an immigrant family's infant daughter share the story of how the baby was almost thrown overboard when fear spread that she might be ill with cholera. Sudden improvement lead the anguished mother to realize that the infant was merely sea-sick.

F.A.S.T. BIKE TRAIL (for Fulton, Albany, Savanna, and Thomson) is a 25-mile bike trail being developed on an abandoned Chicago, Milwaukee, and St. Paul rail bed between Savanna and Albany. As of this writing, three miles of the trail are complete between Fulton and Lock & Dam 13. Along the trail, look for cactus flowers which bloom in June in a remnant sand prairie, river views and woodlands. Bike · hike · cross country ski

HERITAGE CANYON HISTORICAL VILLAGE is a private restoration project located near the north end of Fulton's 4th Street in the area of an old abandoned lime quarry. Restored blacksmith shop, country school, village church, log cabin settlement, and both swinging and covered bridges. During the annual *Fulton Fall Fest,* pioneer crafts are featured throughout the canyon village. Free and open to the public year around.

BULGER'S HOLLOW FEDERAL RECREATION AREA (Proceed four miles north of Clinton, Iowa, on *USH 67.* Turn east onto county road.) Small camping area · dump station · picnicking · boat launch

For more than half of the 19th century, great rafts of lumber were maneuvered through the winding Mississippi River by using two towboats. The forward boat would steer, the aft would push.

CLINTON COUNTY, IOWA

Clinton, Iowa
Population 29,201

The town site for this more populous twin-city to Fulton was set when two friends established a ferry service on either side of the river. Like other Iowa cities, Clinton benefitted from its location on the western shore--the expansion side--of the Mississippi River.

The westward movement of the early settlers meant that the larger cities would be located just west of a dividing river or great lake. It simply made more sense to develop industry and distribution centers on the expansion side of the Mississippi. The towns along the western Illinois border were forever overshadowed by their eastern cities--which, too, had been the first cities to supply the western expansion.

It becomes obvious as the traveler crosses the bridge from Fulton onto 4th Avenue, that Clinton is a diked city. Floods in 1885, 1951, and 1965 inundated the town for as much as six blocks inland before the dike was constructed. The Mississippi River has meandered as much as twenty miles inland from its current path. Old river beds provide only tenuous footing for the suburban developments that have paved over the oxbow bottoms. The city is one of the longest on the river, stretching for nine miles along the Mississippi.

Several handsome Victorian mansions and churches overlook the river, including the home of George M. Curtis, an influential "lumber baron" before the turn of the century, and the Unicorn Restaurant and gift shop.

What to see in Clinton

BICKELHAUPT ARBORETUM (340 South 14th Street). A collection of more than 2,000 plants, 600 trees, and a prairie restoration project. Education center and tours.

CLOWN MUSEUM (Located at the Masonic Temple, 5th Avenue South and lst Street. *Open only during Felix Adler Days, the 3rd weekend in June).* Commemorates the 50-year career of Clinton native, *Felix Adler* as a Ringling Brothers clown. Inducted into the Clown Hall of Fame at Delavan, WI, in 1989, Adler performed in every city of over 500 population in this country.

Adler's favorite prop was a pig named *Amelia* and he trained over 350 young "Amelias" during the course of his career. Adler also trained a dog to latch onto his baggy clothing and not let go until Adler quit kicking. On one occasion, Adler was hoisted to the top of the tent with the dog clamped tight to his leg. When the equipment malfunctioned, Adler kept kicking until safely back on the ground so that the dog would not fall to its death. Adler also wrote many of the scenes from the *Three Stooges.* For information on the museum or Felix Adler Days, call 319-242-5412.

The Ringling Brothers held their first "penny or pin" performances in McGregor, IA. La Crosse, WI, hosts an annual international *Clown Camp.* Baraboo, WI, is home to the *Circus World Museum.*

CURTIS MANSION (420 5th Avenue South). Restored Queen Anne style home of George M. Curtis, co-founder of the Curtis Woodworking Factory and a U.S. Congressman from Iowa. National Register of Historic Places.

Clinton was a lumbering town from the mid-1800s to 1905. Previous to that it had abundant flour mills which were easily converted to sawmills as the "breadbasket" moved north. It has been said that most of the lumber for frame houses on the prairie came through Clinton. After the lumber boom, mills continued to produce fine furniture and decorative wood pieces.

EAGLE POINT PARK AND NATURE CENTER (North 3rd Street). 200-acre city park with observation tower overlooking the Mississippi River. Playground · picnicking · cross-country skiing · children's zoo

HISTORICAL SOCIETY MUSEUM (708 25th Avenue North). A fine local history collection. Note especially photos depicting widespread flooding in the city and the lumbering heritage of Clinton. A lithograph in the museum shows a to-scale birds-eye view of the city when lumber was floated from the north in vast rafts. Lumber yards, mills, and rafts claimed virtually the entire river frontage.

The freelance artists who made this and other aerial views of towns during the 19th century never actually saw the towns from this angle. It was created entirely from observations made by walking around the streets of a town. They envisioned the perspective in their minds and were remarkably accurate. *(See the lithograph of Davenport and Arsenal Island, page 89)*

CLINTON AREA SHOWBOAT THEATRE The restored steam paddlewheeler is permanently dry-docked in Riverview Park. Professional summer stock theatre from June through August. The boat's engine room is open to visitors.

Like Savanna to the north, Clinton was a major interchange for railroads traveling north-south and east-west. The extensive train yards are located at the south end of town. Every thirty minutes, passenger trains arrived in Clinton from throughout the surrounding area. Such easy access made Clinton the "Opera Town of the West." Entertainers famous throughout the world eventually found their way to Clinton. The Historical Museum includes a display of autographed photos from many of them.

RIVERBOAT GAMBLING cruises aboard the *Mississippi Belle II* are available at the riverfront. Weekend casino cruises between Clinton and Bellevue, IA, provide an excellent opportunity to experience the river in a most traditional style! For current prices, boarding, and cruise schedule call 800-426-5591.

RIVERVIEW PARK, Clinton's well-developed riverfront, is home to Riverview Stadium and the *Clinton Giants,* a Class 'A' ball team affilicated with the San Francisco Giants. A 1.6 mile recreational trail on top of the levee has been named the *Discovery Trail,* to commemorate two astronauts (Pinky Nelson and David Hilmers) from Clinton who manned the first Discovery mission. A third astronaught from Clinton County, Dale Gardner, is also flying space shuttle missions. The trail offers hikers and bikers a chance to visit one of the numerous islands off the Clinton riverfront. The three lighthouses along the waterfront were constructed by the W.P.A. in the 1930s.

SPECIAL EVENTS

Fulton Fun Days, Fulton, first weekend in May. Traditional Dutch costumes, dances, food.

Art in the Park, Clinton, mid-May. Over 100 artists and craftspeople display artwork in Lyons Four Square Park.

Felix Adler Days, Clinton, 3rd weekend in June, Clinton. Clown gathering, activities, competitions, performances, photo opportunities.

Riverboat Days, Clinton, July 4th week at Riverview Park. Parade, carnival, entertainment, water shows

Fall Festival, Fulton, 2nd weekend in September. Early American crafters recreate a pioneer settlement at Heritage Canyon. Civil War reenactment.

Duck Fest. Thomson, first weekend in October

Annual Eagle Watch, Lock & Dam 13. January

Clinton to Camanche, Iowa (3 miles)

The drive to tiny Camanche (pronounced CAH-MANCH) on *USH 67* is distinctive for its low-lying nature. There are no limestone bluffs in view, and the highway itself follows an elevated causeway. The name Camanche was intended to refer to the *Comanche* Indians, but was misspelled in the platting.

To continue south to Princeton, IA, and the Quad Cities, see Chapter 6, page 71. Chapter 5 follows Iowa's Great River Road north from Sabula to Dubuque, IA.

Sand dredged from the main channel forms an attractive recreational island. When possible, such dredge material (called "spoil") may also be deposited on shore to form beaches or to be used as fill in public projects.

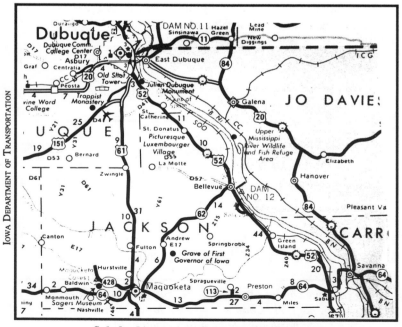

Sabula, IA, north to Dubuque, IA (Chapter 5)

JACKSON COUNTY

Sabula to St. Donatus, Iowa

Woodland Indian Mounds still dot Iowa river bluffs where several more recent Native American tribes including the Fox (or Mesquakie), Sac (Sauk), Illinois (Illini), Winnebago, and Iowa (Iowaye) Sioux were competing for prominence upon the first arrival of Europeans. In 1833, American settlers poured into Iowa to stake a claim in the newly designated Black Hawk Purchase after the final battle of the Black Hawk War in Victory, WI.

Many river towns were established by enterprising claimants who crossed the river by canoe, rafts, or log-- whatever would get them to the other side the fastest. The claims, however, were not legalized until land sales began in 1838 at which time there were already 22,000 people living in the state. Government land grants sold for $1.25 an acre.

In 1837, the final year of President Andrew Jackson's term, Jackson County joined the Wisconsin Territory by authorization of the Wisconsin Territorial Legislature. The tiny town of Andrew, located midway between Bellevue and Maquoketa, completes the commemoration of the president who signed into law the Wisconsin Territory.

There are several Jackson County historical museums located near the Great River Road. *Sagers Museum,* near *Maquoketa Caves State Park,* has an outstanding collection of Native American artifacts. The *Young Museum,* Bellevue, includes a large collection of Parian glassware and other objects collected by the Young family from around the world. The *Gehlen House Doll Museum,* St. Donatus, contains over 4,000 dolls. The main county collection is located at the *Jackson County Historical Museum* in Maquoketa.

Sabula, Iowa
Population 710

Upon crossing the bridge from Savanna, IL, to Sabula, IA, the traveler is following the same route Isaac Dorman did in 1835, though he is one who kicked his way across the river clinging to a log. The rather unusual name, Sabula, is from the Latin word *sabuluum* meaning sand.

While Sabula today is gleefully described as Iowa's only "island city," easily accessible by bridge, boat or causeway, that is only a recently accurate description. Before 1937, it was a flood-prone agricultural center on the Iowa shore, transacting much of its trade with Savanna, IL.

When the U.S. Army Corps of Engineers began development of the lock and dam system, it became apparent that the flatlands surrounding Sabula were destined to flood, as did nearly 200,000 acres of lowland along the upper Mississippi River. The carefully designed system of levees, causeways, and lakes which now protect the 150-year old town provide both water control and recreational benefits.

The levee drive around the city provides convenient opportunities for watching waterfowl, eagles and hawks, and other bottomland bird life. The levee park with picnic tables and park benches encourages at least an hour or two of "down time." A convenience store, large campground, boat launch, and marina cater to the numerous fishermen, hunters, trappers, and campers who delight in the river-oriented "getaway" that Sabula offers. Several lovely stone homes dot Front Street which faces the Illinois shore.

Sabula and causeways seen from the air.

SOUTH SABULA LAKES PARK AND CAMPGROUND (Broad Street, located at the southern-most end of the island). Operated by Jackson County. Picnicking · fishing · boat launch · playground · electric hookups · dump station

JACKSON COUNTY WELCOME CENTER is located on the Iowa mainland at the intersection of *STH 64, USH 67,* and *USH 52.* The building is a replica of a 1-room country school and is open year around. Be sure to note the metal artist's interpretation of Jackson County history from early natives to the present day. Visitor information · giftshop · restrooms

> 18 miles south to Clinton, IA, on *USH 67*.
> 21 miles north to Bellevue, IA
> 44 miles north to Dubuque, IA

USH 52 north to Bellevue winds through vast, secluded bottomland with occasional rock outcroppings. While the road is excellent, there are few amenities until Bellevue. Notice the levee which protects the fields from flooding, though the river itself is one to three miles to the east. There are no bridges crossing the river between Savanna and Dubuque, a distance of 44 miles.

MOONEY HOLLOW DANCE BARN has as its landmark a silo cleverly disguised as a big fiddle. Dances and live performances throughout the year. *USH 52* continues to meander through the unIowa-like ridges and hollows of this unglaciated portion of the state.

GREEN ISLAND STATE WILDLIFE REFUGE (just north of Mooney Hollow, 8 miles south of Bellevue). 3,500-acre waterfowl refuge is a "sleeper"--a cluster of wilderness lakes and sheltered backwaters (a canoeist's paradise) abloom in season with waterlilies; myriad flora and fauna, wetlands that have been compared to the lower Mississippi River delta region. Canoe access to Green Island backwaters and the Maquoketa River. Primitive camping allowed in the refuge · scenic overlooks · picnicking · fishing · cross-country skiing

The tiny, faded settlement of Green Island sits along a brooding wall of sandstone about one mile east of the highway turnoff to the refuge--along with an abandoned railroad track, a church, and a teeny-tiny post office which is now closed. Return to the main highway and continue to the north. Low bluffs and rock outcroppings continue to the west, and, just south of Bellevue, river views to the east.

BELLEVUE STATE PARK, DYAS UNIT (south of Bellevue on *USH 52.*) This state park has two units, *Dyas and Nelson,* separated by the 2-mile wide floodplain of the Maquoketa River. Nine miles of foot trails, scenic overlooks. Camping·electricity ·showers· dump station·cross country skiing·picnic sites·scenic overlooks· nature trails

This blufftop portion is named for the Dyas brothers who received a large land grant in the area as a military bounty after the Black Hawk War. In winter, bald eagles concentrate near the open waters below Lock & Dam 12. Pileated woodpeckers, hepatica blooming in early spring, Jacob's Ladder, and the smooth cliffbrake fern complete the picture.

PLEASANT CREEK FEDERAL RECREATION AREA (3 miles south of Bellevue on *USH 52.* One of several very well maintained Army Corps of Engineers campgrounds, Pleasant Creek also shelters the northern-most stand of pecan trees in the Western Hemisphere. Camping · fishing sites · boat launches · scenic river-level views · hiking · cross country skiing · playgrounds·water·dump station

DUCK CREEK COUNTY PARK, located two miles south of Bellevue on *USH 52,* between the two units of state park. Tent camping · fishing

MILL CREEK COUNTY PARK, south edge of Bellevue on *USH 52.* Creek runs past historic *Potter's Mill.* Boat launch into the Mississippi River. Fishing·picnicking·water·no camping

BELLEVUE STATE PARK, NELSON UNIT. Located atop a 300-foot high limestone bluff with panoramic views of the Mississippi River valley and Lock & Dam 12. An informative nature center and the largest *Butterfly Garden* in Iowa. Hiking · scenic overlooks · picnicking · cross-country ski · easily accessible Indian Mounds · playground · no camping

Bellevue State Park Overlooking Lock & Dam 12

BUTTERFLY SANCTUARY

The *Garden Sanctuary for Butterflies* contains over 100 separate plots, each featuring plants which provide nectar for adult butterflies and/or host plants for caterpillars. Pathways allow visitors to enjoy the wide variety of butterflies and flowers. An area has been established next to the garden to allow close-up viewing of the butterflies.

According to the Iowa Department of Natural Resources, butterflies found in Iowa are either in the process of migration or are completing one of the various stages of their life cycle. Approximately 60 species of butterflies can be expected to make their appearance at the Butterfly Garden each year. Host plants for butterflies include wild aster, ragweed, goldenrod, lambsquarters, daisy fleabane, milkweed, cottonwoods, wild cherry, hackberry, and willows.

Bellevue, Iowa
Population, 2,240

Bellevue is French for "beautiful view" though the little town with the giant view up and down the Mississippi River was actually named for John Bell, who submitted the plat for *Bell View* in 1835. Bellevue, like Dubuque and Davenport, received special charter status as one of the first five cities in Iowa. White settlers arrived in 1833. The claim of one early settler, William Dyas, is still family-owned.

Several historic homes are open to the public as Bed and Breakfasts, including The *Dyas House,* located on the south end of Bellevue, and *Mont Rest,* a Queen Anne restoration complete with wrap-around porch, tower, and turrets which provide panoramic views of Lock 12 and the river. *Springside,* at the north edge of town, offers an excellent opportunity for the traveler to experience an overnight in an 1840s stone mansion. The beautiful Gothic Revival home is on the National Historic Register. Illuminated at night, it is clearly visible from the Great River Road and the river.

RIVERVIEW PARK runs nearly the length of town, has a gazebo, and offers a mostly unobstructed view of the Mississippi to both the north and south. Walkway leads to a new floating public dock adjacent to stone warehouses originally built for Jasper's Flour Mill. A public boat launch is available.

IOWA RIVERBOAT GAMBLING began in 1991, and the *Mississippi Belle II* docks at Riverview Park. The elegant 500-passenger floating casino operates a regular weekend cruise between Clinton and Bellevue. Call 800-426-5591 for details.

LOCK & DAM # 12 (located just north of Bellevue). Visitors are welcome to watch barges and boats lock through. Parking area beside the lock makes it easy to observe right from your car.

POTTER'S MILL (below state park bluff alongside Mill Creek). The original proprietor, E. G. Potter, walked the Mississippi River shore from St. Louis to St. Paul looking for

the perfect location for his flour mill. He must have chosen well, as Jasper's Flour Mill operated as a working merchant grist mill for 126 years, from 1843 to 1969. The Arnold Reiling family purchased the mill from Potter in 1871 and operated it until 1921. Carefully restored it is now one of fewer than 50 mills still in existence in Iowa. It houses a gift shop and a fine restaurant offering lunches, dinners, and Sunday brunch.

MINDY BROWN

Inside, the atmosphere and workings of Iowa's oldest frame mill have been preserved. Ask for a copy of the self-guided tour.

"Its history has really consumed me," muses manager and preservationist, Dan Eggers. "Though I am a sculptor at heart, it is in restoring these historic buildings that I satisfy that creative urge."

THE BELLEVUE WAR

While it has been suggested that the states of Illinois, Wisconsin, and Missouri began with a distinctly north/south orientation, the infant state of Iowa did not. This was a *western* state, and, in the 1840s, Bellevue seemed to shelter more than its fair share of cattle thieves and outlaws.

Apparently, many of them once worked under the protection of a Philidelphia immigrant, William Brown. Mr. Brown not only owned the main hotel and meat market but was also the elected town magistrate.

The Bellevue War, a gun battle between Brown's gang and the more upright citizens of Bellevue, resulted in more deaths (seven) than any other western shoot-out in history.

At the end, trapped in the burning hotel, those members of the gang not shot to death leaped from flaming windows. Some escaped, never to be seen again. Captured outlaws were put in a skiff with three days rations and set adrift on the Mississippi. Almost twenty years later, several of these were accused of the senseless torture and murder of Col. George Davenport, who, along with Antoine Le Claire, platted the city of Davenport, IA.

Two plaques commemorating the Bellevue War can be found at the corner of Riverview and Jefferson Streets. The battle is reenacted the first May weekend of each year during *Bellevue War Day.*

SPRUCE CREEK PARK (located 2 miles north of Bellevue off *USH 52).* A major county campground and recreation area. Fishing·boat launch·picnicking·playground·cross-country ski · complete camping facilities

One now climbs up out of the river valley. Upland views prevail until the Luxembourg settlement called St. Donatus comes into view beyond John Henry Weber Park.

JOHN HENRY WEBER PARK (located at the top of the hill 4 miles north of Bellevue on *USH 52*) is named for the pioneer explorer and trapper for whom Colorado's Weber River, Weber Canyon, Weber State College, and Weber County were named. Weber headed one party of the Ashley-Henry exploration of the Missouri River Basin in the early 1820s and returned to live his final 15 years in Bellevue. Hiking · scenic overlooks · picnicking · toilets

FRITZ CHAPEL HISTORIC SITE is a small wayside chapel about 3 miles west on a gravel road. **Not developed.** Commemorates the safe passage of an early immigrant family across the Atlantic ocean.

SPECIAL EVENTS

Way of the Cross Pilgrimage, St. Donatus, Calvary Hill. Good Friday.

Bellevue War Day, Bellevue. 1st Wknd in May. Reenactment of historic shootout. Food, entertainment.

Heritage Days Fest, Bellevue. 4th July Weekend. Flea market, dance, ski show, food, fireworks.

Buckskinner's Rendezvous, Bellevue. Last Weekend in July. Commemorates trapper John Weber.

Pro Rodeo, Bellevue. Mid-August

Painting of Bellevue by N.D. Shahrivan

St. Donatus, Iowa
Population 140

A small white chapel in a distant sheltered valley is the first glimpse for the traveler of one of the most picturesque villages along Iowa's Great River Road. Currently, 34 stone buildings in St. Donatus (locally pronounced *DO-NAY-TUS*) are on the National Register of Historic Places. Another 50 stone buildings have been recorded in the surrounding countryside.

Constructed between 1830 and 1850, the stone homes and public buildings of St. Donatus are considered to be the best collection of Luxembourger stonework extant in the new world. Watch for the distinctive notched roofline and stucco exterior walls of the original buildings. The stucco served to protect the stonework and mortaring, though some people are now removing the stucco to display the skillfully crafted stone-work below. Several buildings, noted below, are open to visitors.

Be sure to visit the *Lower Town,* a cluster of old buildings off to the left/west of the Gehlen House. *Tête-des-Morts Creek* seems a gentle little stream here, but note the flood wall protecting homes along the roadway--the creek has flooded to that point within recent memory. The haunting remains of an old stone mill show, too, that the creek has shifted well away from its earlier track.

A Brief History of St. Donatus

Tête-des-Morts Creek was named by Father Louis Hennepin whose party had paddled off the Mississippi River and into the creek to find a grisly sight--skulls placed on sticks barricading the creek. Apparently the victors of an Indian battle had driven the vanquished warriors backward over the bluffs, dashing their bodies on the rocks below. The victorious tribe stuck the losers' skulls onto sticks, thus the ghastly appellation *Tête-des-Morts* meaning "Heads of the Dead."

The Iowa *(or Iowaye)* Indians, a breakaway group of the Sioux nation, inhabited the area at the time of the French explorers, but they were already feeling pressure from eastern groups such as the Mesquaki (Fox), Sac, and Winnebago Indians, who were being forced west by Europeans and Americans. The Sac and Mesquakie eventually settled into the Iowa counties of Jackson, Clinton, and Scott, plus several counties to the west. It is possible that the battle at Tête-des-Morts Creek was between the Iowaye Sioux and the Sac/Mesquakie Indians.

Corn, beans, and squash would have been raised in the fertile flood plain while the men hunted for game, and fished for fish and mussels in the nearby streams and the river.

Tête-des-Morts Creek winds its way to the Mississippi River through the privately owned *Ni-Da-Ho valley*. The bluff described in the story of the Indian battle still guards the creek's entrance to the river. A regional artifact collector is believed to have accumulated one of the largest personal collections of fossils and Indian/French artifacts in the world. Many are displayed at the Sager Museum.

The mouth of Tête-des-Morts Creek is just upriver of the Galena River mouth which facilitated commerce between the two river towns. In 1838, the ferry fee to cross a team of horses and a wagon was $2. An individual rode for 25 cents, cattle for 50 cents a head.

Places to Visit in St. Donatus

KALMES Restaurant and Olde Tavern (located on *USH 52* across the street from the Gehlen House and Barn) offers the visitor a chance to hear the local Luxembourg dialect. In the winter, lessons in the Old World tongue are given by towns-people to keep the strong Luxembourg heritage alive. Kalmes has been a family business since 1850.

THE GEHLEN HOUSE is a fine example of traditional Luxembourg architecture. Look for a distinctive notch at the roof ends and stucco covering the locally quarried limestone blocks. Built in 1848, the National Register building also serves as the village visitor information center and houses the doll museum and an antique collection.

The Gehlen Barn has a gabled rather than notched roof line and likely predates the 1840 arrival of the Luxembourgers. In his notes, Julien Dubuque mentions a French settlement on Tête-des-Morts Creek at the south end of his Spanish land grant.

Gun slots are clearly visible to the south and west of the Gehlen Barn

The Gehlen Barn, believed to be the oldest building in St. Donatus, is being privately restored by owners Betty and Harold Fondell. Early settlers would have lived in the top level of the barn, the animals below. Note the gun slots, in the south and west walls, intended as a defense against Indian attacks. The Fondells were largely at the heart of the effort to have St. Donatus placed on the National Register. It is only during the past five years that *any* public funding has been available to save the 150-year-old structures.

ST. DONATUS CATHOLIC CHURCH, to the east of Gehlen House, was built in 1858 and restored in 1907. It houses a beautifully carved, German Baroque alter. The parish center contains a heritage museum. The historic cemetery has French, German, and English inscriptions, and unusual stones, wood and metal markers. Donatus was a Roman soldier who became the *Patron Saint for Protection from Thunderstorms.* Yes, storms can be quite severe throughout this central portion of the Mississippi River valley!

THE HISTORIC OUTDOOR WAY OF THE CROSS is accessed by a path located next to the cemetery. Built in 1861, it is the oldest outdoor Way of the Cross in the United States. Its fourteen stations, each with a tiny wayside chapel, wind switch-back style up *Calvary Hill.* Crowning the hill is the simple *Pieta Chapel,* built in 1885. On Good Friday, 700 to 1,000 people make their way up Calvary Hill to the chapel.

The view from the hilltop looks out across the peaceful valley to the twin spires of St. John's Lutheran Church. Catholic Luxembourgers settled on one side of the valley, German Lutherans on the other.

THE STONE HOUSE on the hillside beside the Catholic church was once home to the first boys' school in Iowa.

INSIGHT

Elizabeth Fondell
Preservationist

"*The restoration of the Gehlen house and barn has really been our life's work. It has suddenly dawned on Harold and me that our entire family life and family savings have gone into preserving those buildings. Vacation time, vacation money, weekends. My goodness, even the grandchildren are growing up, and we're still working on those buildings. No, it's time to move on, to visit our grandkids, do some traveling.*

"*A lot of energy went into researching the old construction techniques. How did they formulate the limestone mortar? Were the gunslots really a type of ventilation system? What was the original purpose for that pile of stone rubble beside the barn. The barn still looks old, but so much has been redone; rebuilding the upper walls, the entire roof, the lofts. It's a labor of love to do it with integrity.*

"*I think our interest in architectural preservation was kindled back when the Convent School for Girls was torn down. It was a magnificent structure! A four-story high, classic stone building, with the distinctive Luxembourger notches in the roof line. The School Sisters of Notre Dame had maintained it for over 100 years, but when the school closed, the parish decided that maintaining the building would be too costly. The Order left town a few years later.*

"I always had a feeling that we owed them more than that. Perhaps our effort to preserve the remaining buildings is a kind of thank you to them. It's difficult, though, to lead a preservation effort. You're always coming into conflict with someone. You're always agitating. You can't be timid."

THE U.S. ARMY CORPS OF ENGINEERS

Pleasant Creek and 24 other public recreation areas are maintained by the Rock Island District U.S. Army Corps of Engineers along a 314-mile stretch of river from Guttenberg, IA, just north of Dubuque, to Saverton, MO. These recreation areas are located on public land acquired by the federal government in the 1930s as part of the Upper Mississippi River 9-foot commercial navigation channel project. (Although this author has described this area as the *Middle* Mississippi, it is officially regarded as part of the Upper Mississippi.) Most of these areas are open year-round and offer camping, picnicking, fishing and boat access to the river. There is a 50% discount on the already reasonable camping fee for citizens over age 50.

Navigation charts showing the locations of stump fields, wing dams, islands, and the 9-foot channel are available for a nominal fee by writing: U.S. Army Engineer District, Rock Island, P.O. Box 2004, Clock Tower Building, Rock Island, IL 61204-2004.

After St. Donatus, the Great River Road climbs steadily into the agricultural uplands above Dubuque. Chapter 6 continues from Clinton south to the Quad Cities.

OUR LADY OF THE MISSISSIPPI ABBEY (8400 Abbey Hill). Located riverside of the Great River Road, east onto Hilken Road at the sign indicating an Abbey. The Trappistine Sisters produce and sell an excellent caramel candy. From the ridgetop, there is a grand view of surrounding agricultural land.

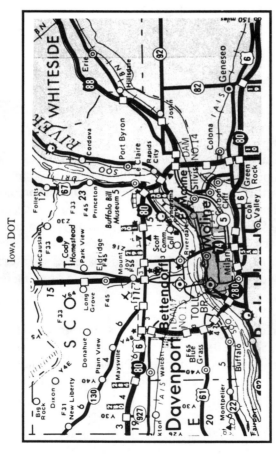

Folletts to Buffalo, IA, including the Quad Cities

SCOTT COUNTY, IOWA

The Quad Cities

The broad river valley between Folletts and Princeton, IA, was scoured out by the *Wapsipinicon River* (locally pronounced WAP-SEE-PIN-I-KON) which was named for two Indian lovers (Wapsi and Pinicon) who leapt to their deaths from bluffs further inland.

The Wapsipinicon River carries a steady stream of silt which then settles in the slower moving current of the Mississippi River. Piles of *spoil* (mud and sand dredged from the 9-foot deep shipping channel) are visible along the shore north of Princeton.

U.S. Army Corps dredge boats can be identified by a floating tail of hose, illuminated at night, which carries the spoil "vacuumed" from the river bottom to the sandpiles located on nearby riverbank or islands. Princeton's large sandy beach is formed from this dredge spoil. *(See photo, p. 52)*

BUFFALO BILL BOYHOOD HOME (Located 4.7 miles east of Long Grove, off *USH 61*. Twenty minutes north of the *I-80*. Open 9 a.m. to 6 p.m., April through October.) The boyhood home of *William F. Cody (Buffalo Bill),* famous government scout and wild west showman, is located up the Wapsipinicon River. *See also the museum in Le Claire.*

Princeton, Iowa
Population 806

Travelers from northern stretches of the Mississippi River will find that Princeton feels a lot like home after the lowland drive from Savanna. Homes are set into a scenic limestone ridge, and numerous large stone warehouses and former hotels cluster around the riverfront.

The riverside bank in Princeton sports a steamboat decor and a large collection of local and riverboating memorabilia. The only bank on the upper Mississippi River to advertise *banking-by-boat,* it is owned by the grandson of a steamboat captain who was specially licensed to run riverboats through the rapids between Davenport and Le Claire.

The drive from Princeton to Le Claire is one of the prettiest thus far in the trip. Natural rock gardens, vacation homes, and open water sparkling below. The river here remains open even during the winter due to the warm water discharge from the Cordova nuclear plant on the opposite shore.

Until this point the river and the ridges have been encased in graying February ice and snow, but here the river sparkled in the sun and created an instant, unexpected, feeling of summer vacation in the middle of winter. Open water on a sunshiny day is a sure cure for any Northerner feeling the effects of cabin fever.

QUAD CITIES NUCLEAR POWER STATION (Visitor Center is located on Illinois *STH 84* near Cordova, IL.) Open Tuesday through Sunday. Displays on the operation of a nuclear power plant.

Although it is only eight miles to Bettendorf and the Quad Cities, there is little urban sprawl as yet from that population center of nearly 400,000 people. Notice the pitch black soil, rich prairie loam which has made Iowa the most agricultural state in the union.

> **8 miles to Bettendorf, IA**
> **11 miles to Davenport, IA**

MISSISSIPPI VALLEY WELCOME CENTER (3), Le Claire, IA. Completed in 1989, this *Iowa Welcome Center* offers not only tourism information but also interpretive displays of local history and natural history and an Iowa gift shop. The Welcome Center overlooks a 6-mile wide view of the Mississippi River Valley and resembles a Victorian-era riverboat captain's home.

Le Claire, Iowa
Population 2,734

Much of the pleasure of traveling along the Great River Road lies in exploring sedate little river towns along the way. Turn off *USH 67* and stroll along Le Claire's riverfront. There you will find a paddleboat's view of the town's *Front Street,* with old warehouses and tenements of the river-oriented commercial district. Victorian mansions look out over the town from atop the ridge. The riverfront includes the inevitable railroad tracks, picnic tables, and a paddleboat. A restaurant overlooking the river makes this a particularly pleasant stop.

A Brief History of Le Claire

This little river burg was originally platted by *Col. George Davenport* and his business partner and government Indian interpreter, *Antoine Le Claire,* in 1834. The site was one of two awarded to Le Claire as payment for his services during negotiations for the *Black Hawk Purchase.* The second site was platted by the two men in 1838 as the City of Davenport.

Le Claire is situated at the top of what was once a 14-mile long rapids (one of the longest river rapids in the world) that began just below Davenport.

Until the first river lock and dam (# 15 in Davenport) was built in 1934, the fluctuating river depth often required freight and passengers to transfer from large river boats to smaller ones with a lesser draft which could run the rapids. At best, even in high water, specially licensed (and especially well-paid) pilots were required to maneuver safely through the rocks in the river. Nineteen of these specially licensed pilots lived in the city of Le Claire.

BUFFALO BILL MUSEUM (2) (200 N. River Drive, Le Claire, IA). Historical look at riverboat history and the life and times of Buffalo Bill Cody, wild west showman and Le Claire native. Open seasonally.

LOCK & DAM 14 (southwest of Le Claire, off *USH 67).* Observe American bald eagles in open water below the lock and dam during the winter months. Restrooms · picnicking · observation deck

335 miles to Minneapolis, MN
163 miles to Chicago, IL
240 miles to St. Louis, MO

THE QUAD CITIES

In truth, the metroplex that is often referred to as the Quad Cities (referring to Davenport and Bettendorf in Iowa, and Moline, and Rock Island, Illinois) consists of fourteen smaller communities in addition to five larger centers (including East Moline). Davenport is the largest with a population of 95,300. Rock Island, originally platted by Col. George Davenport as *Stephenson,* is the oldest. The area encompasses a population of 400,000, most of which is concentrated within three miles of the Mississippi River.

Parkhurst and Port Byron, IL, became established upriver of Davenport; Buffalo and Rockingham (on the Rock River) to the south. Camden (now *Milan* -- and pronounced MY-LAN) was named after a prominent Philadelphia suburb and opened to settlement in 1843 with a dam supplying power for two flour mills and a saw mill. A side trip to Cordova's riverfront might be rewarded not only with a great river view, but an outstanding homemade dessert at McCool's cafe.

Early investors believed that, located at either end of the rapids, any of the settlements might prosper by catering to overnight passengers and supplying goods and services to others who would have to stop while arrangements were made to navigate freight over the rapids.

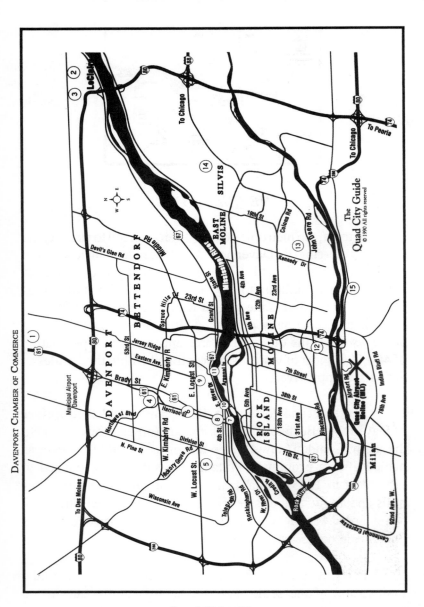

Quad Cities Map

This was an area Mark Twain described as *"bristling with great towns projected the day before yesterday--and built the next morning. "* Sales to New York City agents for land in Rock Island "City" generated $500,000 for Col. Davenport in 1837. By 1839 only two homes had been built and it was proclaimed one of *"many humbugs palmed upon the public in the way of towns and cities in the far west. "*

Today, the economy revolves around tourism, finance, agriculture, food processing, machine and weapons manufacturing, and aluminum roll processing. *(Much of this local history is from* **The River and The Prairie,** *a book by Dr. William Roba.* © *1986 by The Hesperian Press.)*

What to See in the Quad Cities
(Numbers, when noted, keyed to City Map)

If time permits, plan at least an overnight in the area. History from the period of *western expansion (1816-1860)* abounds. There are several excellent museums which interpret Indian and military history in the area. Several B&Bs are located in historic districts while interesting boutiques make a visit to the *Village of East Davenport* a "must." Art museums, harness racing, professional sports, and abundant cultural events will round out the visit very nicely.

Visitors will find travel throughout the Quad Cities area to be very manageable thanks to several interstate highways which intersect at the city. The most confusing element will be plotting directions. The Mississippi River flows from northeast to southwest through the cities. Speaking in terms of "up river" and "down river," rather than "north" or "south," is the first step to finding one's way around the Quad Cities.

Bettendorf, Iowa
Population 28,432

Upon entering *Riverdale,* just outside the metropolitan area of Bettendorf, the huge all-aluminum exterior of the ALCOA Aluminum Plant is the most distinguishable of several heavy industrial plants located along the Iowa shore. It is the largest aluminum rolling plant in the world.

STEAMBOAT LANDING is an expansive recreational facility adjoining the *Diamond Lady* riverboat casino. With a spritely calliope, high fluted smokestacks, and a bright red paddlewheel, the elegant floating casino is a replica of the flagship of the historic *Diamond Jo* Steamboat Company. Tickets and boarding areas are located just below the *I-74* bridge at Riverside Park. For current scheduling information, please call 1-800-322-4FUN.

The scenic four-hour cruise to or from Muscatine includes "locking through" two of the Upper Mississippi's 27 locks. Cruise prices vary depending on which meals are included. Meals are excellent.

THE CHILDREN'S MUSEUM OF BETTENDORF (just off the Great River Road at 2215 16th Street) is a pleasant family stop. The hands-on museum offers numerous action displays for children. The local history section has displays of Indian artifacts and explains the unusual *onion farming* history of the area. By 1920 the area had been renamed for the Bettendorf brothers who employed 3,000 men in the Bettendorf Axle Co. The revolutionary 1-piece axle can be examined on the railroad car in the yard. Picnic tables on the grounds. Open Tuesday through Saturday, 10 a.m. to 4:30 p.m. Sunday 1-4 p.m. Donation.

Moline, Illinois
Population 43,202

The industrial city of Moline is located just across the river from Bettendorf on *I-74 East*. It is considered to have the third largest Belgian community in the U.S. and is home to a Belgian government Consul. The name Moline is derived from *moulin,* the French word for mill.

It was the manufacturers who came first to Moline after David B. Sears built a 600-foot dam from the eastern edge of Rock Island (Arsenal Island) to the Illinois shore in 1837. The dam united the island and the mainland, providing power for saw mills, grist mills, foundries, a machine shop, cabinet factory, and finally--lured by the promise of a new frame building and free water--John Deere's plow shop.

DEERE AND COMPANY HEADQUARTERS (13)   John Deere Road, Moline, IL. John Deere was a blacksmith from nearby Grand Detour, IL. Deere developed the first plow capable of plowing through the thick prairie loam without gumming up. It had a super-slick or ''self-scouring'' steel blade rather than the pitted iron plows then being used.

The Deere and Company Administrative Center, designed by the late Eero Saarinen (who also designed the Gateway Arch in St. Louis) has been described as the ''Versailles of the West.'' Locals will recommend that if you can see nothing else, see this.

The product display building includes the *Girard Mural,* made up of more than 2000 historical items from the period 1837-1918. Open daily to 5:30 p.m. Guided tours conducted Monday-Friday at 10:30 a.m and 1:30 p.m. Free.

Rock Island, Illinois
Population 40,552

The city of Rock Island is located directly opposite Davenport and just off the west end of the rocky island (Arsenal Island) for which it was named. *Centennial Bridge* connects the two cities for a 50 cent toll. There are numerous walking tours and B&Bs located in the historic areas between 19th and 23rd Streets and 1st through 14th Avenue. Printed guides describing the historical and architectural walking tours are available at the Quad Cities Convention & Visitors Bureau, 1900 3rd Avenue, Rock Island.

Potter House B&B, Rock Island

As a testament to its early Swedish population, the Swedish Lutheran Augustana Synod moved both its headquarters and *Augustana College* from Chicago to Rock Island in 1869. The home of *Frederick Weyerhauser,* who developed the lumber industry in Wisconsin to supply his saw mills in Rock Island, is still located on the campus grounds.

SUNSET PARK (located northwest side of Rock Island) River side park and overlook. Fishing · boat launch · picnicking

CASINO ROCK ISLAND at the Boatworks brings riverboat casino gambling to the Illinois shore in March 1992. Call 800-477-7747 for complete information and schedules. There is no loss limit on Illinois-based boats and minors are not allowed on board.

LONGVIEW PARK (located on 17th Street and 18th Avenue) is situated on the original pasturelands of the Davenport family estates. Extensive city park with panoramic views of the river. Public swimming pool · tennis courts · picnicking

BLACK HAWK STATE HISTORIC SITE (1510 46th Ave [Black Hawk Rd]). Displays at the *Hauberg Indian Museum* interpret the daily life of the Sac and Mesquakie (Fox) Indians living in the area from the 1730s to the 1830s. The massive stone and timber lodge was built by the *Civilian Conservation Corps* during the 1930s. Open daily year-round. Free.

The 208-acre park and nature preserve adjacent to the museum offer hiking trails of moderate difficulty along the steep banks of the *Rock River* and through a mature oak-hickory forest. Visit the prairie restoration behind the park office and the historic *Dickson-Sears Cemetery* on the north side of the park. Interpretive walks and programs are offered throughout the year.

One cannot help but be conscious, when walking through the park, that here was Saukenuk, homeland of the Sac Nation. On these same grounds overlooking the Rock and Mississippi rivers were perched the lodges, the campfires, and the cornfields that Black Hawk, Keokuk, and the people of the Sac nation had loved and fought for in the early 19th century.

Black Hawk Portrait
1837 by Chas. Bird King

A *Very* Brief History of the Sac Nation

The Sac and Mesquakie (Fox) Indians who played so prominent a role in Iowa and Illinois history were not native to the banks of the Mississippi River. Pressured by Europeans and eastern Indians moving into their native hunting grounds at the lower bay of Lake Michigan, the two Indian bands gradually pushed their way west between the Wisconsin and Rock rivers. About 1730 they settled near the confluence of the Rock and Mississippi rivers.

The Sac village of *Saukenuk* encompassed the ridge and lowlands between the Rock and Mississippi rivers and was one of the larger Indian settlements on the upper Mississippi. It was home to a population of 5,000 to 8,000 Sac and Mesquakie, including the future warrior-chiefs, *Black Hawk* and *Keokuk*. Saukenuk was burned by American soldiers during the American Revolution in retaliation for Indian cooperation with the British. The skirmish is considered to be the furthest north and west in the War for Independence.

The village of Saukenuk included Rock Island (now *Arsenal Island)*, located three miles north of the Rock River confluence, and *Credit Island,* a neutral trading site for Indians and trappers alike located just down river from Davenport. Campbell Island, just north of Rock (Arsenal) Island, was named for Lt. John Campbell, who was attacked and soundly defeated there in 1814 by Sac warriors.

By 1828, Keokuk had moved south to the Iowa River, and Black Hawk had begun agitating for the return of the Illinois homeland fraudulently obtained by the American government in 1816. Eventually, Black Hawk was forced to flee the American forces, leading his warriors and their families north his warriors and their families north into Wisconsin and then looping back along the Wisconsin River toward the Mississippi River in an effort to return to the west bank.

In the battle of the Bad Axe River near Victory, WI, the starving band was massacred as it tried to escape to the west bank across the maze of Mississippi River islands.

Black Hawk and his war have been commemorated up and down the river. Every town has its Black Hawk park, hotel, saloon, museum, or cafe. Gen. Winfield Scott (for whom Scott County was named) participated in negotiations with Keokuk and Wapello to end the war. The resulting Black Hawk Purchase in 1832 opened for settlement 6 million acres of land in Iowa and Minnesota for little more than $130,000.

"Settling the Black Hawk Purchase, " Painting by Dorothy Proksch. The stone marker still stands hidden in the grass alongside Wisconsin's Great River Road. It reads, "On the eve of August 1, 1832, Black Hawk and his men, with a flag of truce, went to the head of this island to surrender to the Captain of the steamer, Warrior. *Whites on the boat asked, "Are you Winnebagoes or Sacs?" "Sacs," replied Black Hawk. A load of canister was at once fired, killing 22 Indians suing for peace.*

Davenport, Iowa
Population 95,300

In 1816, George Davenport set up business as a *sutler,* providing amenities for the soldiers stationed at Fort Armstrong. By 1819 he and his partner, Antoine Le Claire, controlled trading from Des Moines to Dubuque and recorded doing a gross business of $10,652 with 195 Indians. To the north, Joseph Roulette controlled trading between Dubuque and St. Anthony Falls (soon usurped by Hercules Dousman of Prairie du Chien) while August Chouteau controlled the fur business out of St. Louis.

Portions of St. Anthony's Church (named to commemorate Antoine Le Claire) date from 1838. The church is located at the corner of 4th and Main streets. Davenport's home on Arsenal Island is being restored and may be toured.

Davenport boasts nineteen distinct historic districts on the National Historic Register. The *Village of East Davenport* and the *Bridge Street* historic districts located just upriver of downtown Davenport along the Great River Road are most conveniently located for the visitor. Be sure to glance up at the "Quality Row" of magnificent Victorian mansions which overlook the Village. Davenport's parklike riverfront is located right where the river makes its "big bend" to the west.

Local B&Bs provide the visitor with an opportunity to spend the night in a lovely restored Victorian home. Contact the tourism bureau for an updated listing of B&Bs and other historic districts throughout the Quad Cities.

THE PRESIDENT (7), which docks at President's Landing in Riverview Park in Davenport, is the largest floating casino on the upper river. Built in 1924, the sidewheeler was the largest overnight passenger steamer operating on the Mississippi River. During the early 1930s it was purchased by Strekfus Steamers (the *J.S.* and the *Capitol)* in St. Louis and has since been rebuilt of steel to operate with a diesel engine. *The President,* now completely renovated to feature 27,000 square feet of casino gaming space, has been classified as a National Historic Landmark. For current information, call 1-800-BOAT-711.

PALMER COLLEGE OF CHIROPRACTIC (Brady Street between E. 10th and 11th Streets). B.J. and Daniel Palmer were, respectively, the father and the developer of the chiropractic profession. Both were lifelong residents of Davenport. *B.J. Palmer* was a man of many interests and talents, developing the chiropractic college in 1895 and establishing the first radio and television stations in the state of Iowa. B.J. wrote 38 books on numerous topics from health to travel. *The Putnam Museum* contains a large portion of his personal collection of Oriental/ Egyptian artifacts.

PUTNAM MUSEUM (5) 1717 West 12th Street. An outstanding museum of regional natural history and heritage. One of the better river views may be seen from the museum. Permanent American Indian and Quad Cities historic exhibits focus on the past 12,000 years. Tuesday through Saturday 9 a.m. to 5 p.m. Sundays 1 to 5 p.m. Family rate $6.00.

DAVENPORT MUSEUM OF ART (5) Adjacent to the Putnam Museum at 1737 West 12th Street. Permanent collection of 19th and 20th century American art. The Regional Collection focuses on *American Gothic artist Grant Wood.* Tuesday-Saturday to 4:30 p.m. Sunday 1-4:30 p.m. Free

FEJERVARY PARK (5) and VANDER VEER PARK & CONSERVATORY (6) are major Davenport city parks. Playground, bison, deer, and wild turkey are at Fejervary Park near the Putnam Museum. Vander Veer's floral conservatory dates from 1897. The *Rose Garden* features 1800 roses of about 145 varieties.

ADLER THEATRE, RIVER CENTER (8)   136 E. 3rd St. Davenport. Beautifully restored art deco theatre.

VILLAGE OF EAST DAVENPORT (9) Delightfully restored shopping area has a bakery, restaurants, and numerous specialty shops ranging from used books to birdseed and Christmas decorations.

This historic retail area dates to 1851 and was built on the site of Camp McClellan, a Civil War mustering and training camp for Union soldiers in Iowa. The annual Civil War reenactments and the Stubb's Eddy River Buckskinners' Rendezvous are well worth attending. James Stubb was a soldier from Ft. Armstrong who lived a hermit-like existence in a cave beside an eddy in the rapids for twelve years--long enough for the rapids to become known as Stubb's Eddy.

NIABI ZOO (15) Coal Valley, IL. Quad Cities Zoo includes over 400 mammals, birds, and reptiles from around the world. Open mid-April to mid-October until 5 pm. Small Fee

ARSENAL ISLAND

The largest of three river islands located within the Quad Cities is Arsenal Island. Long known as Rock Island, it provided both a promontory on which to locate *Fort Armstrong* in 1816 and a huge cave, now flooded, wherein dwelled the Great Spirit of the Sac nation.

In 1856, the first railroad bridge to span the Mississippi River was built from Arsenal Island to the City of Davenport-- the narrowest span on the Mississippi River. When the steamer *Effie Afton* promptly crashed into the bridge pilings and burned, the steamer sued the infant Chicago and Rock Island Railroad for impeding navigation on the waterways. Abe Lincoln, a young country lawyer from Illinois, made a national name for himself by successfully defending the right of railroads to build bridges across the Mississippi River.

The judge in this landmark case apparently had to agree with his simple logic that, *"A man had as much right to cross a river as had another to travel up and down a river."* A piling from this first bridge still sits at the edge of Arsenal island. It is marked with a bronze plaque and surrounded by pine trees.

Today, Arsenal Island is home to one of the largest Army munitions arsenals in the U.S.A., employing as many as 10,000 civilians during peak periods. Currently, approximately 4,000 civilians pass through the check gates each day.

The main access is via *Government Bridge* at the east end of the island. Built in 1895, the *iron swingspan bridge* consists of a lower level for cars and an upper level for trains. As boats entering the lock and dam at close range have right of way, bridge traffic must stop while the bridge swings open to allow boats to pass through the lock. Visitors will enjoy the levee walk and numerous historical stops on the island.

LOCK AND DAM 15, ARMY CORPS OF ENGINEERS VISITOR CENTER (10) *The Rock Island District Office of the Army Corps of Engineers* is housed on Arsenal Island. The new visitor center allows an opportunity to see the operation of Lock and Dam 15 at close range. *Be sure to examine the excellent model of the staircase effect which the lock and dam system imposed on the Mississippi River.* The visitor center is open 9 a.m. to 9 p.m. May to September. Visitor Information · restrooms · picnicking

RESTORED HOME OF COL. GEORGE DAVENPORT The newly restored woodframe house looks out over the Mississippi to the City of Davenport. Here the area's first permanent settler platted out Davenport with Antoine Le Claire. It was here also that Col. Davenport was tortured and murdered in 1845 by a group of river bandits looking for gold. Davenport is buried at historic *Chippiannock Cemetery* in the city of Rock Island. Home tour is free, 1-3 p.m. on weekends.

BROWNING ARSENAL MUSEUM (11) Building 60. The second oldest army museum (after West Point) in the nation interprets the history of Arsenal Island from Indian times to the present; including a model of old Fort Armstrong, an extensive military firearms collection, and an explanation of manufacturing processes at the arsenal. Over 75,000 horse harnesses were produced here during World War I. Other displays pertain to the Black Hawk War and the Confederate prisoner-of-war camp housed on the island. 10 a.m. to 4 p.m. Free.

Many of the sandstone buildings on Arsenal Island date to the 1860s and are used by the U.S. Army Armament Munitions and Chemical Command for manufacturing, engineering, research and development. A public BIKE/HIKE trail tops the levee which surrounds the island.

NATIONAL CEMETERY (11) There is both a Confederate and National military cemetery on Arsenal Island. Nearly 2,000 of the 12,000 Confederate prisoners held at the POW camp during the Civil War died from measles and small pox. The rows of tidy white markers carry the names of regiments and, occasionally, individuals: Mississippi Regiment, Alabama Regiment, Florida Regiment, Virginia Cavalry; W.A. Harper, Georgia Cavalry; Jessie Mues, Missouri Cavalry. . . *Because dogtags were not then in use, almost a third of the soldiers who died in the Civil War were never positively identified.*

CREDIT ISLAND PARK (just downriver of Davenport on the road to Buffalo). Causeway access through wet bottomlands. Named by the fur traders who preferred Credit Island to the larger Arsenal Island for transacting business with the Indians. Good birding, waterfowl. Ball diamond·playground·picnicking

Aerial view of Davenport and Arsenal Island is typical of lithographs produced by freelance artists in the late 19th Century.

SPECIAL EVENTS

Stubbs Eddy River Buckskinners Rendezvous. Village of East Davenport. Third Weekend in May. Buckskinner camp. Pioneer (1830-1860) food, crafts, games, and storytellers.

International Woodcarvers Congress, Davenport. Late June. Master woodcarvers display and competition.

Mississippi Valley Blues Festival and Great River Ramble. Events located throughout the Quad Cities area. First weekend in July. National, international artists. One of the top Blues Festivals in the nation combines with the Quad Cities 4th of July celebration. Venetian boat parade, food and beverages, hot air balloon races, parades, fireworks.

Bix Beiderbecke Memorial Jazz Festival. Davenport, Le Claire Park. Late July. One of the nation's largest jazz festivals commemorates Davenport-born jazz musician, Leon "Bix" Beiderbecke.

Civil War Muster & Mercantile Exposition, Village of East Davenport. Mid-September. Civil War buffs re-enact actual battles of the Civil War. Approximately 500 soldiers, both blue and grey. 19th century merchants in Sutler's Row. Crafts people and artisans demonstrate traditional crafts. Lady's Tea and military ball.

The Messiah, Augustana College in Rock Island. Mid-December. Handel's classic work has been performed annually since 1882.

American bald eagles are abundant at Credit Island and above the open water below the dam during the winter months. While as many as 200 eagles have been observed fishing here in recent years, Rachel Carson could find only 59 of them during a count in the 1950s. The resurgence in the eagle population has been largely due to the ban on DDT and other harmful pesticides since the 1960s. Please, do not worry wintering waterfowl as they work hard just maintaining body heat. Any additional stress is life-threatening to them.

CAMPING IN THE QUAD CITIES AREA

PORT BYRON (The town of Port Byron was named for the romantic poet, Lord Byron) City Boat Launch.
Seasonal camping at Camp Hauberg *(STH 84 North)* 150 sites
· boat launch · fishing · swimming · playground

DORRANCE FOREST PRESERVE *(STH 84* and Hillsdale Road).

FISHERMEN'S CORNER Federal Recreation Area (1 mile north of Hampton, IL, on *STH 84,* adjacent to Lock & Dam # 14). Water · boat launch · picnicking

ILLINIWEK FOREST PRESERVE (near Fishermen's Corner Federal Recreation Area). 80+ sites, most with electricity and water.   Historic bridge and scenic overlooks.   Playground · boating · picnicking · hiking

LOUD THUNDER FOREST PRESERVE (7 miles west of Andalusia, IL, on *STH 92).* 167-acre, man-made lake with river access from 5 launches in the area. Fishing · boating · boat rental · concession stand · camping · hiking · horseback riding

BLANCHARD ISLAND FEDERAL RECREATION AREA (1.5 miles east of the Muscatine bridge on *STH 92.* Turn south on black top road. Proceed 4 miles. Turn right onto secondary county road and proceed west to the levee). Picnicking · water · dump station · boat launch

ON THE ROAD TO BUFFALO

> **Buffalo, IA 5 miles**
> **Muscatine, IA 24 miles**

The decision to continue along the Great River Road to Muscatine, IA, involves the choice of either the Illinois or Iowa shore--an excellent opportunity for each traveler to do a little independent "research" over coffee and eggs at the corner cafe.

"Well," you're likely to learn, *"there's several small towns that haven't changed that much in the last 100 years, except that the old corner grocery's been replaced by a new Seven-Eleven."*

Or, *"Andalusia, IL, is a nice little historic river town and that Loud Thunder Preserve is really fantastic!"*

And as often as not, *"Actually I've never been on the River Road, but let me call my mother-in-law's sister--she's from Muscatine and probably knows someone who lives along the river. It'll only take a minute!"*

IOWANS HAVE TO WIN THE PRIZE FOR OUT-AND-OUT FRIENDLINESS!

> This route will follow the Iowa shore along *STH 22* to Muscatine, then cross the bridge on *STH 92* to Illinois, meander through Illinois' rural Henderson County, then return to Iowa at Burlington on *USH 34*.

The main shipping channel of the Mississippi River is adjacent to the Iowa shore during the short drive to Buffalo, IA. Grain elevators, chemical factories, cement companies, and rock quarries are situated along the shore for easy loading and unloading onto the commercial shipping barges. Between March and October, each tow with a crew of eleven can push enough freight in 15 barges to fill twenty fully-loaded freight trains.

Buffalo, Iowa
Population 1,260

With its historic business street still aligned along the riverfront, Buffalo is one of those "little-changed" river towns. The town sits on a broad flat plateau just opposite two long river islands. Founder Benjamin Clark used the opening between the islands to lay claim to the area which, in 1833, became the first settlement in Scott County. It was named to honor the hometown of Clark's partner.

Like many Iowa towns, Buffalo boasts its own writer, George Cram Cook. Cook and his wife, Susan Glaspell (a Pulitzer prize winning novelist and playwright from Davenport) started the Provincetown Players at the tip of Cape Cod in 1915.

There is also a *Quaker* (Religious Society of Friends) church in Buffalo, a reminder of the influence of Quakers who moved into the area, particularly neighboring Cedar County and west to Iowa City, during the mid-19th century. The son of one Quaker family in West Branch, *Herbert Hoover,* went on to become the 31st President of the United States. His birthplace cottage and one of America's eight presidential libraries is located just north of *I-80,* at exit 259. In Cedar Rapids, just north of Iowa City, the Quaker Oats Cereal Company became one of the largest cereal mills in the world.

BASIL WILLIAMS

Several different religious sects settled along the Mississippi River in the mid-1860s, each hoping to practice religious beliefs in peace. Today artist colonies have developed in the Amana Colonies, IA, and at the former Swedish commune at Bishop Hill, IL. The former Mormon community of Nauvoo, IL, is the largest restoration project in the Midwest.

INSIGHT

Isreal (Issy) Joseph Gorman
Oiler aboard The President

"There ain't nothin' aboard this boat that I can't fix. It was Capt. Roy Strekfus, the owner of the J.S. *and the* Capitol, *and the* President, *that made sure I could do everything. I started out polishin' his shoes when I was eleven years old and he hired me on as his cabin boy. I'd come down to the* President *every time it was in New Orleans. I'd beg them to take me on, but they always said how I was too young, there wasn't nothing for me to do. But Capt. Roy saw me, how this scrawny little kid kept comin' down to the boat, and he had me sent up to his cabin.*

"Can you polish shoes?" he asked.

"Oh," I told him, "Yes, sir!" and he took me on for $12 a week. I been on this boat since 1939! I know everything about everything, from them engines to the kitchen. That's the way Capt. Roy wanted it. I'm the only one with a permanent room on the boat. It's always been my home. I got a beautiful family, too, in New Orleans. A fine woman and seven kids, too. So I guess I got home often enough!

"Oh, I've been on the river a long time and seen lots of changes. For one thing, the river is a lot safer to travel on. Putting in the locks and dams, dredging, cleaning out the snags. The boats are so much bigger today than they were. So much more freight is carried. And the river ain't nearly as dirty--or smelly with all that black smoke from hundreds of boats. As boats were loaded and unloaded, anything that was damaged just went into the river: boxes, bananas, garbage. It was full of garbage. Between that and the smelly smoke. . .it's just a lot cleaner now."

"Another year and I retire. I'll head back to New Orleans. Yes, sir, I took care of the boat and the boat took care of me!"

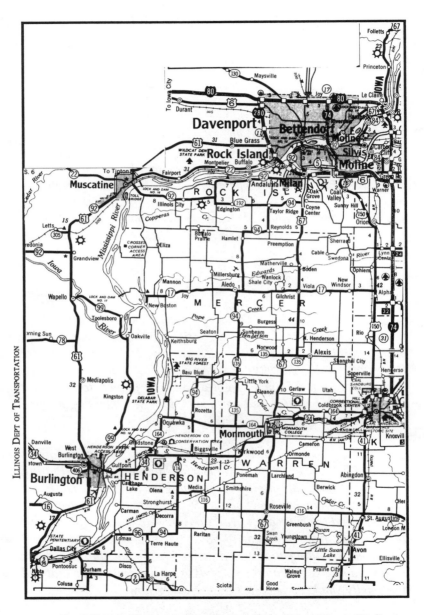

Quad Cities to Muscatine, IA (Chapter 7), and Muscatine to Burlington IA, via New Boston through Oquawka, IL (Chapter 8).

MUSCATINE COUNTY

Montpelier to Muscatine, Iowa

Located just five miles downriver from Buffalo on *USH* 22 is the "new" village of Montpelier (locally pronounced MONT-PILL-EE-ER). Originally situated at Wild Cat Den six miles further down river, it was the first settlement in Muscatine County. The business district at Wild Cat Den gradually shifted toward the new railroad depot at what is now Montpelier. The original passenger depot has been moved off the track and restored as *Varner's Depot Bed & Breakfast*.

This portion of Iowa's Great River Road, was constructed as a W.P.A. project during the 1930s. Stories persist that it was so hot during construction that horses commonly died in their harnesses, to be dispatched into the ditch and quickly replaced with fresh stock.

BUFFALO SHORES ACCESS AREA. A large marina with excellent camping facilities.

CLARK'S FERRY FEDERAL RECREATION AREA provides pleasant bottomland camping just at the south end of town. The name commemorates Capt. Benjamin Clark, though locals are quick to point out that Clark founded Buffalo, not Montpelier.

There are no restaurants or shops in Montpelier, so campers should be well supplied before arriving. Be cautious at the unguarded railroad crossings. As many as 26 Burlington Northern freight trains pass along the river road each day.

WILDCAT DEN STATE PARK (follow the signs off *STH 22* several miles southwest of Montpelier) protects the townsite of Muscatine County's first settlers. It was here that Benjamin Nye established his grist mill on Pine Creek in 1848. There is a picnic area on the mill site, where the restored mill, its water wheel, and the dam are still in place.

The infrequent mail delivery to Nye's 1838 general store and post office was addressed simply: *Iowa Post Office, Black Hawk Purchase, Wisconsin Territory.*

One can still cross the bridge over the creek, visit the school house (both built in early 1880s), and wander through the historic cemetery. The original Methodist church, built of native stone by German masons, is located about two miles beyond the mill site and now belongs to the Muscatine County Historical Society.

The state park has an onsite ranger, several camping areas, and extensive hiking trails through a variety of terrain. 75 foot sandstone cliffs and outcroppings provide scenic overlooks. 25 varieties of ferns have been found in Wildcat Den.

The densely wooded hillside opposite Pine Creek is a portion of the Wildcat Den State Park wildlife refuge. The blacktop road winds up the hillside, past the park campground near the top of the hill, and on to the old general store and Lutheran Church of the teeny-tiny settlement of *New Era.*

In the small white Lutheran Church across the street from Kemper's General Store, Vincent Gilbert, a master restorer of pipe organs, worked steadily as he extolled the virtues of the New Era pipe organ.

"You'll seldom see such a beautifully carved case, and two faces are displayed to the congregation! Every one of the 600 pipes is a "speaking" pipe. Stand in that corner! Just listen to this low C!" I sense--not hear--a low reverberating rumble.

He wishes only that I could play so he could stand in a corner and listen. *"Listen to it from the altar,"* he suggests, *"the resonance in this church is remarkable!"*

Tomorrow his name plate will go onto the keyboard and the vast unseen workings of the pipe organ will become, officially, a Gilbert organ. A theatre organ in a tiny white church to be rediscovered by another generation--when not only the original craftsmanship but also the restorer's work will be admired anew.

I spoke with Ted Kemper, nearly 80, and his wife, who was still tending the little general store. Ted had clear blue eyes but he was a little stiff this day as his wooden leg was giving him some trouble. He seems bemused to think that after all these years it is a memory of a soggy Sunday morning that still comes to mind.

INSIGHT

Ted Kemper
New Era, Iowa

"*My grandpa Kemper received most of the land in this area in a land grant. My mother came from Hamburg, Germany, where they had a small farm. There were mostly German settlers in the area. Some of them were stone masons who built different things, like the Methodist Church. Our German cousins used to come to work on the farm over the summer. I did some commercial fishing and hunting. We packed the fish into iced barrels to go to Chicago. We did the same with rabbits.*

"*Grandpa had a choice one time of buying more pasture land up here or buying the Village of East Davenport for the same price. He chose the adjoining pasture land as it required a day's drive by wagon just to get to East Davenport from Montpelier.*

"*The Lutheran Church was designed by an architect from Chicago, the brother of the two ladies who built the church and this store. Their money came from a baking powder patent. I've heard that through the grapevine. The pipe organ was put into the church in 1914, and it's costing about $15,000 to restore it.*

"*Something I remember clearly about being young was the eight mile horse ride to the second Methodist church. Eight miles was a comfortable distance because a man on horseback could go eight miles in an hour. Twenty miles was too far. It could take a horse with a wagon all day to go twenty miles.*

"*Anyway, I was in some Sunday School program on a day when it was just pouring rain. Of course, the whole family went anyway. The horse and I went the distance through the rain as fast as we could, but the family rode in an open wagon. We all got sopped. I still remember that.*"

FAIRPORT CAMPGROUND (6 miles downriver from Wildcat Den State Park on *STH 22)*. 44 sites along the Mississippi River. Electricity · dump station · boat ramps

The road to Muscatine is built on a levee well up from the level of the fields. The stilted cabins are perched remarkably high. There will be no docks along the Mississippi here as the water level fluctuates wildly.

SHADY CREEK FEDERAL RECREATION AREA (1.5 miles east of Fairport off *STH 22)*. Picnicking · boat launch · camping · no electricity · dump station

THE FAIRPORT STATE FISH HATCHERY (8 miles northwest of Muscatine). Formerly a U.S. Fish and Wildlife Service Hatchery for spawning large mouth and small mouth bass, blue-gills, sunfish, and channel catfish, it is now operated by the State of Iowa. Picnic areas. Tours possible.

SAULSBURY BRIDGE RECREATION AREA (Located on Cedar River, 8 miles northwest of Muscatine). 675 acre nature complex for recreation, hunting, wildlife management.

200 miles to Chicago
48 miles to Burlington
100 miles to Dubuque
307 miles to Minneapolis/St. Paul, MN
253 miles to St. Louis

Muscatine, Iowa
Population 22,881

Located at the site of a *Mascoutin* Indian village and platted as Bloomington in 1836, the present city name was set as Muscatine in 1849. The name provided a link with the original Indian village, yet was determined by the Post Office to be more easily spelled than Mascoutin (often misspelled as Moscouten, Moscoutin, Mascouten, etc.) The Indian word may be translated to mean "prairie" or "burning island." The latter may well be a reference to the Indian practice of burning off the high grass from Muscatine Island.

At the junction of *STH 22* and *USH 61* in Muscatine, a right hand turn leads to the shopping mall and modern motels. *USH 61* south passes the Norbert Beckey Bridge to Illinois and through the downtown Muscatine business district to a well-developed riverfront. The *Diamond Lady* riverboat casino offers a four-hour cruise to Bettendorf which passes through two river locks.

WEED PARK (northeast section of Muscatine, just off *STH 22)* is a large city park donated by James Weed in 1907. Lagoon · fishing for children · outdoor swimming pool · playground · concession stand·picnicking·ball fields·tennis·Indian mounds · Mississippi River views

MUSCATINE ISLAND (south on *USH 61).* Open-air farm markets mid-July through October offer fresh fruits and vegetables, locally made crafts, and other souvenirs. Muscatine is well-known for its huge, delicious *Muscatine muskmelons.*

LOCK & DAM 16 (.6 mile east off *STH 92,* across the Norbert Beckey Bridge and turn left onto the first road). Public tours every Sunday afternoon. Observation deck·restrooms·picnicking

MARK TWAIN OVERLOOK (just off *USH 61,* 1 block northwest of the Norbert Beckey Bridge into Illinois). View of the Mississippi River, bridge, lock & dam, and boat harbor. Restrooms · picnicking · historical marker with information on the overlook and the *National Great River Road*

In 1854 Mark Twain joined his brother, Orion in Muscatine, where Orion had purchased a partial interest in the *Muscatine Journal.* Twain wrote of the sunsets there, *"I have never seen any on either side of the ocean that equaled them."*

LAURA MUSSER HOUSE MUSEUM AND MUSCATINE ART CENTER (1314 Mulberry Avenue). Beautiful mansion dating from 1908 houses local history collection. One room in the museum is devoted to the pearl button industry and the collection includes two originals by Mississippi River panorama painter, *Henry Lewis.* The art center is adjacent to the museum and features revolving displays of contemporary art.

The Muscatine Prairie, painting by Henry Lewis.

HENRY LEWIS
Mississippi River Panorama

While visiting the Laura Musser House Museum, note the two original paintings by St. Louis panorama painter, Henry Lewis. While Lewis was only one of many panorama painters competing for audiences and display area during the late 1840s, he often claimed to be the first to conceive of painting the entire Mississippi River, from St. Anthony Falls to the Gulf of Mexico.

The original 4-mile long canvas has been lost, but Lewis also published a book which reproduced the main pictures from the panorama. These full-color plates have been reproduced along with many of Lewis' observations and personal letters in *Mississippi Panorama,* a book by William Peterson. The book is still available from many regional bookstores and museums. It offers a fascinating visual record of life along the Mississippi River in 1848-49. The *Piasa Bird* picture page 216 is also reproduced from that collection.

The concept of a panorama had been perfected in 1846 to the point where as much as 4 miles of canvas could be unrolled from a huge upright roller on one side of the stage onto a huge roller on the other side. Viewers would sit as in a theatre while the panorama unfurled before them. Most of these huge dioramas have been lost.

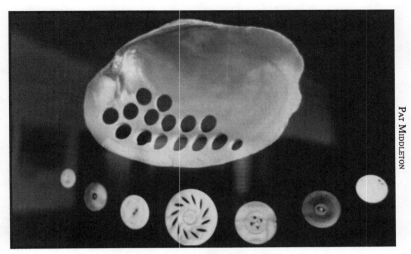

Holey Clam Shell with Pearl Button Samples

A Brief History of Muscatine and the Pearl Button Industry

Like Davenport, Dubuque, Bellevue, and Burlington, Muscatine is one of Iowa's five original Charter Cities. Like those cities, its largely German citizenry profited from the lumber boom in the late 1800s and from a very early railroad link with the Quad Cities and the east/west railroads. Col. Davenport located a trading post here in 1833. In 1835, James Casey began servicing riverboats with cord wood and by 1839, 71 people and 33 buildings had sprouted near "Casey's Wood-pile."

In 1884, a German by the name of J. F. Boepple founded the Mississippi River pearl button industry by applying his native trade to the abundant Mississippi mussels. By 1890, Muscatine was known as the *Pearl Button Capital of the World* employing 2,500 workers in 43 different button-related businesses.

Factories in Muscatine received the rounded blanks cut from clamshells from as far away as Prairie du Chien, WI, and Louisiana, MO. Much of the machinery used in the button industry was invented and manufactured in Muscatine. An outstanding collection of samples and memorabilia (including some of the early button making equipment) from the pearl button industry is on display at the *Laura Musser House Museum.*

In addition to forming buttons, the iridescent Mother-of-Pearl lining was shipped by boatloads to Germany for $125/ton. There, craftsmen inlaid the shell into knife and gun stocks, jewelry boxes, furniture, and other items.

The tiny bits of pearl found in many shells were disparaged by buyers as *chicken feed* or *slugs,* but were, in fact, quite valuable in Europe when formed into jewelry. On occasion, the rare, perfectly formed pearl found by a clammer on the Mississippi might bring $1,000 from a local pearl buyer and finally be sold in London for $50,000.

Today, Muscatine still has several button companies that have since made the switch to plastic buttons. Engineering/architectural consulting, grain processing, the Heinz ketchup plant, and the HON office equipment company remain the economic bulwark of the area.

MERCER AND HENDERSON COUNTIES

New Boston to Oquawka, Illinois

Located along the Illinois shore of Pool 18, Mercer and Henderson counties represent vintage Illinois prairie and river flood plain. State Highways *17* and *164* cross through vast, flat fields of melon, corn, and other vegetables. In a gentle breeze, the ripe smell of hogs sweeps across the highway. *(See map on p. 96)*

The riverside towns of New Boston, Keithsburg and Oquawka, IL, were long referred to by local Sac and Mesquakie Indians as *Oquawkiek* or "Yellow Banks" for the landmark yellow sand banks clearly visible to river travelers in this area.

New Boston, Illinois
Population 750

"Be sure to visit New Boston," was the gentleman's advice at the Davenport cafe. "It has a great commercial fish market and the streets were laid out by *Abraham Lincoln.* While the streets seem to be disturbingly off-kilter at various points, Abe's platting has been recently verified. Abe was off by no more than 1/2 to 1 inch!" And so a new character enters the river stories along America's Great River Road.

Abraham Lincoln, 1809-1865
16th President of the United States

This, one soon finds, is Abe Lincoln country. Lincoln, who made his home near Springfield, Illinois' capital city, often criss-crossed the river valley working first as a surveyor, then practicing law before the Court in Oquawka.

Abe was a close friend of the Phelps family of Oquawka and invariably stayed in their home when working in the Yellow Banks area. For surveying New Boston, he might have been paid $3/day; for smaller jobs, a couple of buckskins, a pig, or a meal. At these rates, the $1,100 debt Lincoln had incurred from a failed store in New Salem must have loomed large.

The old town of New Boston, platted by Lincoln in 1834, extends south of Main Street. An historical marker at the corner of Main and Third Street commemorates his handiwork. A pleasant riverside camping area and boat access, an antique shop, a supper club overlooking the river, and two tiny local cafes complete New Boston's visitor amenities.

Several large 19th century houses remain in New Boston, relics from early settler families and busier days. Steamboats moved freight; and vegetable canneries, button factories, and commercial fishermen provided abundant employment. Business partners, Gideon Ives and Elmore J. Dennison, built the twin Italianate homes at Jefferson & Locust in 1857.

STURGEON BAY PARK provides bluff-top camping between the railroad tracks and Good Street within the New Boston city limits. Open April 1 to November 1. There are two boat accesses from the park; a third is located at the foot of Main Street. Camping for approximately 250 units. Electricity · water · sewer · boating · fishing

The Black Hawk War

It was just across the Mississippi River from New Boston that Keokuk and Black Hawk gathered 3,000 warriors to determine whether they would pursue Keokuk's plan for diplomacy or follow Black Hawk and clear the white man from their fields of maize. The pow wow was attended by several members of the Dennison family of New Boston who recorded much of the heated debate between Black Hawk and Keokuk.

Keokuk saved the majority of the Fox and Sac from extinction when he responded eloquently to their heated oratory, *"Yes, I will lead you forth upon the war-path, but on this condition: That we first put our wives and children, our aged and infirm, gently to sleep in that slumber that knows no waking this side of the spirit land...For we go upon the long trail which has no turn...This sacrifice is demanded of us by the very love we bear those dear ones."*

The words were prophetic. Of the 400 Sac warriors and their 1,200 dependents who followed 67-year-old Black Hawk up the Rock River in Illinois, only 150 survived the final massacre by the white soldiers and the Sioux warriors who awaited them along either side of the Mississippi River north of Prairie du Chien, WI. A surviving great-grandchild recently recalled her grandmother's campfire story of how *"the river ran red with the blood of our people."*

While the Black Hawk War which raged in the early 1830s resulted in fear and tragedy for Indians and white settlers alike, there were no skirmishes in the Yellow Banks area. S.S. Phelps of Oquawka did not even feel it necessary to build a fort until 50 drunken soldiers threatened a peaceful Indian chief visiting his home.

Caroline Phelps of Oquawka wrote in her journal, *"My children cried for poor old John, as we called him, as much as though he had been a relative. He was their friend truly. They missed his singing. He used to fix a drum and then drum and sing and have them and the little papooses dance. Anyone could not tell which was which only by their color. Many a time I have went in with all of them singing with blankets on and could not tell my own children. In the evening when they all turned their backs to the door they would all sing alike. My daughter could speak the Indian language just as well as she could her own. But poor John, his friends came and said he was going with his tribe to the Happy Hunting Grounds."*

Other stories circulate about early attempts by Indian braves to either kidnap or purchase young daughters of settlers. Black Hawk himself is reported to have offered first one fine horse, then two, then six horses for the daughter of one the Dennisons. He finally gave up the negotiation, *"more than a little surprised by the high value the white men placed upon their daughters."*

MARK TWAIN WILDLIFE REFUGE, KEITHSBURG DIVISION (located .5 mile north of Keithsburg. 1,452 acres, about 3.5 miles long. Created in 1946 by the U.S. Fish and Wildlife Service to provide undisturbed resting and feeding habitat for migratory waterfowl, also to perpetuate optimum annual production of wood ducks. Open from January 1 to the beginning of the earliest waterfowl hunting season.

> **Muscatine IA, 30 miles**
> **Quad Cities 45 miles**
> **Burlington, IA, 30 miles**

Keithsburg, Illinois
Population 930

A good portion of Keithsburg's commercial district (bounded by Third, Jackson, Fifth, and Washington streets) has recently been placed on the National Register of Historic Places. Most of the buildings in this area date from the mid-to-late 19th century with relatively few alterations.

KEITHSBURG MUSEUM (located on 14th and Washington streets). A driving tour of Keithsburg is available on audio cassette from the museum. Display of local history includes an early pump oil can--invented by A.P. Cannon of Keithsburg to reach all the critical points in the train steam engine. Open summer weekends only or by appointment Wednesday and Sunday afternoons April to November, 1 to 5 p.m.

KEITHSBURG PARK. A well-developed campground and boat access is available to visitors on the riverfront.

The Lighthouse Restaurant is built on two levels: the second level provides viewing over the new levee built to protect the town from river flooding. In 1965, most of the lower portion of town was under 4 to 7 feet of water for almost a month. Row boats provided access to businesses in town. One resident whose home flooded regularly described the river mud at cleanup time as being the consistency of glue. Another flood story described snakes hanging on every available limb and bit of floating debris.

A Brief History of Keithsburg

Like many other small river towns, Keithsburg's economy peaked around the turn of the century. Once home to over 2,000 people, a big weekend in Keithsburg was recorded as having 250 horse teams in town of which 80 stayed over night. Merchants often accepted grain or pork in payment which led to the development of slaughtering and warehousing businesses. A Saw & Planing Mill and lumber yard hoarded the riverfront. A grain elevator, flour mill, cigar factory, and shellers were busy.

In 1838 the train crossed the river just north of Keithsburg, first on a ferry carrying four cars at a time, then on a swing span bridge, then a lift bridge built in 1886. During the winter, passengers might walk or sleigh across the ice. Boaters can see remnants of the crippled railroad lift bridge to the side of the main channel. The old bridge burned after oil was ignited by firecrackers.

The Keithsburg button factory began in 1875 and operated for 55 years. Button blanks were cut from Mississippi River shells, as well as shells shipped in from Arkansas and Wisconsin. Blanks were cut and shipped to Muscatine to be finished into pearl buttons. By-products included chicken feed, fishing bait, and lime dust. The shell debris is known to have been purchased for use as a paving material for roads.

The Keithsburg cemetery includes 135 soldiers from the Civil War. Those who died during the forced march enroute to the POW prison at Rock Island were buried here. (Much of this historical information came from the Sesquicentennial publication of the Keithsburg Historical Museum.)

BIG RIVER STATE FOREST (6 miles north of Oquawka and 4 miles south of Keithsburg, bordering the Mississippi River). Park Headquarters are located near the site of the 100-foot fire watch tower (one of a handful remaining in the state). It is also headquarters for Delabar State Park, Gladstone Lake, Putney's Landing, and other conservation access operations. Camping · equestrian camp · boat access · picnicking · hiking · cross country skiing · snowmobile trails · ten acres of natural prairie

Easily accessible by auto, snowmobile, horseback, or on foot, the flat sand prairie supports a "crossover" of southern and northern flora--most obvious of which is the abundant prickly pear cactus. Other state and federally endangered plants

PRICKLY-PEAR

(large flowered beard's tongue, the Patterson bindweed, kittentails, and flower-of-an-hour) may be found here as well as strawberries and blueberries. Over 200 species of birds have been identified in the park.

Illustration from A FIELD GUIDE TO WILD-FLOWERS OF NORTH-EASTERN AND NORTH-CENTRAL NORTH AM-ERICA © 1968 by Roger Tory Peterson and Margaret Mc-Kenny. Used by permission of Houghton Mifflin Co-mpany. All rights reserved.

Prickly Pear Cactus and other sand-loving flora are found in Big River State Forest

The pine trees growing here were part of a state project begun in 1928 and carried on throughout the early 1940s in an effort to control soil erosion and to demonstrate that pine trees could be a profitable alternative to crops. It has been estimated that sand in the Yellow Banks area averages 300 feet deep, with veins of clay that carry the water horizontally.

BALD BLUFF is clearly visible to the east on the road to the equestrian camp in the Big River State Forest. It is said that Black Hawk ruled all the land he could see from this solitary bluff, including Burlington, Muscatine and Galesburg. It may have been here that he offered his farewell to his land, *"Mine was a beautiful country. I liked my towns, my cornfields, and the home of my people. I fought for it; it is now yours; it will produce you good crops."* An annual commemorative climb to the top of Bald Bluff is held each year during *Heritage Trail Weekend,* the last weekend in September.

THE LINCOLN MILITARY TRAIL (located approximately 1/2 mile from the Keithsburg blacktop, on Bald Bluff Road) is a newly discovered feature of the state forest and is well worth pause. A one and 1/2 mile portion of the trail used by several thousand Illinois troops moving north to the Black Hawk War was only recently discovered by a determined amateur historian, Charles Shinkle. The ancient Indian/settler trail had long been "lost" to historians searching for the route taken by Abraham Lincoln during the Black Hawk War. A small graveyard located on a rise just west of the parking area for the trail contains markers for an 18-year-old woman and a 2-year-old child which date from 1867 and 1873. Signs giving both historic information and directions have been installed.

Abe Lincoln and the Black Hawk War

Abe Lincoln was elected Captain of the Sangamon County volunteers which joined an army of 1,600 soldiers who were mobilized at Beardstown, IL. They marched along the Military Trail in cold, drizzly weather to Yellow Banks on the Mississippi River, then to Dixon and on to Wisconsin. When one company balked at crossing the Illinois border, Col. Zachary Taylor (who eventually directed the final battle at Bad Axe) drew up regular soldiers behind them and gave them a choice between fighting Indians or soldiers--they chose to follow after the Indians. Taylor was elected the 12th president of the United States in 1848.

Abe walked back to Illinois after his horse was stolen near present-day Whitewater, WI. In *The Prairie Years,* Vol. 1 of his epic Lincoln biography, Carl Sandburg notes that though Lincoln had been through an Indian War without participating in a single battle or killing a single Indian, he *had* spent long hours with a volunteer from Springfield who convinced him that he could be a lawyer.

When the Illinois legislature met at the Capitol in 1834, Abe Lincoln was there as an elected representative. He was 25 years old, drawing $3 a day, and wearing a new pair of jeans purchased with borrowed money.

(Sandburg, a major 20th century American poet, was born in Galesburg, Illinois, about 30 miles east of Oquawka. The Carl Sandburg Birthplace Historic Site in Galesburg is open to the public.)

DELABAR STATE PARK (Located 1.5 miles north of Oquawka near *STH 164).* Shaded camping · electric · dump station · water · picnicking · hiking · river fishing

BASIL WILLIAMS

Bridges are almost as varied as bird species on the Mississippi River!

Ice Bridges

Today, bridges provide trains and motor vehicles easy access to the opposite shore. Until bridges began to span the river, however, winter crossings over the river ice was necessary. While common, they were not without peril. In his book *The River and The Prairie,* Dr. William Roba records a journal entry from 1852 which describes the hazards of crossing an *ice bridge.*

"We got down to the shore and found that people had been crossing all the morning on the ice and that it was not considered very dangerous. We got some staffs and started out on a sea of ice for the Iowa shore. We traveled for some distance without any difficulty until we got out over the current where we found the ice piled up on great ledges wedged in all shapes, some

*piled up ten foot high--some immense cakes standing on the edge
with deep chasms between with a swift current of water running
at the bottom.*

*"We went on this way for a long distance, sometimes
leaping from one huge cake of ice to another, slipping and
stumbling every minute until it got so bad that it was almost
impossible to proceed. We looked back and it seemed as far to
either shore as it did from one to the other when we started. The
prospect looked dark and we could not help thinking how
impossible it would be to escape if the ice should break up.*

*"We started on again, thinking we must have gone over
the worst of it and soon we were in Io-way. Just a few minutes
later, Guy heard the shout that the ice was moving. I got up and
looked out and could hardly believe my eyes as I saw the huge
body of ice which we had crossed fifteen minutes before rolling,
tumbling, and foaming in a confused mass as it went thundering
by."*

*Under no condition should those unfamiliar with Mississippi River ice crossings attempt to walk out onto the
frozen river. Unpredictable river currents may leave
only a thin layer of ice or snow in sporadic areas. The
current can eat away ice that was perfectly safe the
previous day. Every year over-confident fishermen,
skiers, and snowmobilers find themselves in the river's
maw.*

THE PHELPS FAMILY
Emigrants Extraordinaire

Stephen Sumner Phelps moved to the Illinois Territory with his family in 1820. Their homestead, near Springfield in Sangamon County, was chosen by brother Alexis who had walked from Palmyra, New York, to Kentucky, through Illinois and back to New York. Steven Sumner Phelps engaged in the Indian trade for his father, north and east of Peoria, IL.

In 1828 Sumner joined his brother in the lead mining rush to Galena, IL, and Dodgeville, WI. A type of lead poisoning made him ill enough to leave mining permanently. Meantime his father had purchased the claim of a Dr. Galland at Yellow Banks for $400. (This Dr. Isaac Galland moved on to Montrose, IA, where he started Iowa's first public school and its first newspaper.)

Sumner and brother, William, set up in *Oquawkiek* with their families and expanded their trading range with Indians in northwestern Illinois and in Iowa. Sumner earned the respect and loyalty of the Indians who called him "Hawkeye."

In 1836 Oquawka was surveyed and the lots advertised as far away as New York City, selling for $900 to $1,000 apiece. The Phelps brothers turned down an offer amounting to $150,000 for their entire claim.

The homes of both Alexis and S. Sumner Phelps still overlook the river in Oquawka. The Alexis home, c . 1833, is being restored by the Henderson County Historical Society. Located between 2nd Street and Hancock, it is thought to have been a stop on the Underground Railroad.

Oquawka, Illinois
Population 1,533

Established as the county seat in 1842, the *Henderson County Court House* in Oquawka dates from 1843 and is the second oldest continuously used court house in the state. Abraham Lincoln and Stephen A. Douglas both gave speeches here when they were campaigning for the U.S. Senate in 1858.

The home of Stephen Sumner Phelps, founder of Oquawka, is located south of Calhoun between Sixth and Seventh streets overlooking a large bend of the river. Abraham Lincoln was a frequent guest at the home which was built in the 1840s.

Before the Henderson County Court House was built in 1843, Circuit Judge Stephen A. Douglas held court at the home of Alexis Phelps, often staying as a guest for the night.

THE GRAVE OF NORMA JEAN ELEPHANT is located at the Village Square between 5th and 6th Streets and Clay and Mason. A circus was in town when Norma Jean was killed by a bolt of lightning on July 17, 1972, while tethered to a small lone oak tree. Permission to bury her was obtained from Springfield, and local citizens contributed money for her interment and monument.

THE OQUAWKA WAGON BRIDGE (2.5 miles south of Oquawka on *STH 164.)* Sometimes called the Henderson or Allaman covered bridge, it was built in 1845-46 and is on the National Historic Register. The bridge washed away during the flood of Henderson Creek in 1982, but with the help of a state grant and many contributions, the bridge was restored and replaced on the original site, using salvaged parts recovered from the creek. The original plans and tools of Jacob Allaman

Henderson County Covered Bridge

were used during reconstruction. This is a lovely picnicking wayside and the only covered bridge found along the Upper Mississippi River.

SPECIAL EVENTS

Delabar State Park Craft Show and Flea Market. Memorial Day Weekend. Beautiful riverside park overlooks and craft displays. Park is crowded. Arrive early to find a site.

Oquawcup Sailboat Race from Keithsburg to Oquawka. Mid-July. Viewing areas at Big River State Forest and Delabar State Park. Race begins at noon.

Heritage Days in Henderson County. Late September: Includes the annual climb of Bald Bluff, located off the northeast section of the Big River State Forest. The highest point in the county, it was here that Black Hawk and his people bid farewell to their land before banishment to Iowa.

Christmas Bird Count throughout Illinois. Last two weeks in December. To participate, call the Illinois Dept. of Conservation, Special Events at (217) 785-8607.

RICH MIDDLETON

Mississippi River author, Pat Middleton (r), visits a shell camp.

Buyers for the Japanese cultured shell industry purchase living and dead Mississippi River mussel (or clam) shells. Shells that were worth a nickel a shell in the late 1970s can now bring from 40 cents to several dollars a pound depending on species and market demand. Shells brought to the shell camp are weighed, processed and shipped. The meats, which are not suitable for human consumtion because of contaminants, are checked for pearls and disposed of.

Independent shellers *(or clammers)* may collect 300 to 700 pounds a day either by dragging a crowfoot bar or diving. Divers using compressed air will crawl around the river bottom or lay flat as they collect shells. Harvesting is done by touch as there is *no* visibility underwater. It is a solitary, dangerous business.

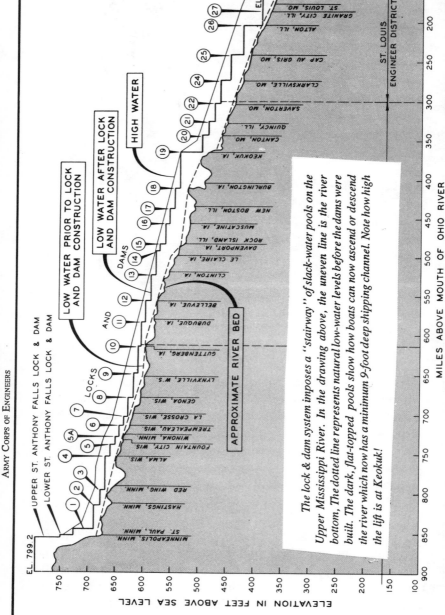

ARMY CORPS OF ENGINEERS

The lock & dam system imposes a "stairway" of slack-water pools on the Upper Mississippi River. In the drawing above, the uneven line is the river bottom. The dotted line represents natural low-water levels before the dams were built. The dark, flat-topped pools show how boats can now ascend or descend the river which now has a minimum 9-foot deep shipping channel. Note how high the lift is at Keokuk!

DES MOINES COUNTY

Burlington, Iowa
Population 27,200

After the flat, sandy prairies of Henderson County, the city of Burlington appears arrayed over a scenic backdrop of low bluffs. The tall steeple of *St. John's Catholic Church* dominates the city's horizon to the southwest. The huge red-tiled building directly ahead is the *Medical Center.* Its mission-style of architecture is unique along the upper river. To the south, the white *Memorial Auditorium* is located in the flood plain along the riverbank.

The *Big Muddy Restaurant* immediately below and north of the bridge is located in the old Burlington, Cedar Rapids, & Northern Railroad freighthouse; expect fine food and river viewing. The *Steamboat Stop Country Store* is located on Main St. between the bridge exit and the Iowa Welcome Center. The building housing this quality gift and craft shop dates from 1841 and, with its plank floorboards and square nails, has changed but little. It is representative of the many tenement homes along the river front which once served as overflow housing for river travelers.

PORT OF BURLINGTON WELCOME CENTER

For the visitor, Burlington's riverside Welcome Center is welcome indeed. Clearly signed, it offers not only a wealth of tourism information on historic Des Moines County, but also a heritage display that includes samples of locally found *geodes* (the state rock of Iowa), and a riverside plaza where one can immediately experience a bit of river-lounging by simply walking outside and leaning against the railing overlooking the Mississippi. The adjacent *Iowa Store* offers quality Iowa products and crafts.

Shoppers will enjoy a stroll along nearby *Steamboat Walk,* a portion of Jefferson Street that has been developed as a walking street lined with trees, shrubs and park benches. Many variety shops line the modern brick street. *Westland Mall* and many motels are located along *USH 34* west. The great rolling prairie of Iowa begins in West Burlington.

That this area has been settled for significantly longer than the farmlands of Wisconsin and Minnesota became immediately clear when I asked a random shopper how long her family had been in the area. She thought for a second and replied that they had arrived in 1793. Her husband and five sons currently run a 100,000-acre corn/hog operation.

A free printed guide to the *Heritage Hill Historic District* is available at the Welcome Center. Here, bounded by Central, High, Third, and Washington streets, are the great treasures of present-day Burlington. The amazing variety of Victorian era homes were built by Burlington's wealthy, late-19th-century businessmen. Wholesalers and distributors, lumbermen, pork processors, and landowners put success on display in commercial buildings and homes sitting proudly on the many hillsides leading from river and ravine.

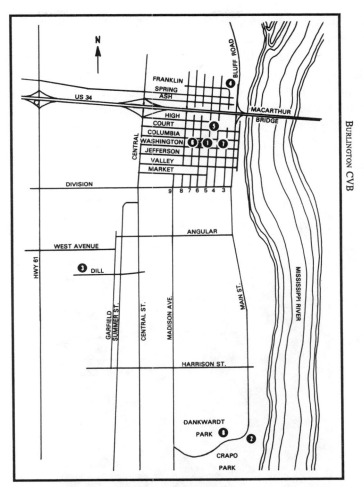

City of Burlington, Iowa

What to See in Burlington *(numbers keyed to city map)*

THE OLD COPP HOUSE *(7)* Located at 4th & one block north of Washington Street. One of the oldest houses in Burlington was built by dry goods merchant, Joshua Copp, from local limestone in 1840. A separate stone ice house sits on the alley.

SNAKE ALLEY *(6),* located between Washington and Columbia on 6th Street, is a "must see." Located on the south side of the Heritage Hill Historic District, it offered businessmen direct access to the business district from their homes on the hill. It has been described in Ripley's "Believe it or Not" as the "crookedest street" in the world. Snake Alley consists of five half curves and two quarter curves over a distance of 275 feet, rising 58.3 feet from Washington to Columbia Street.

RICH MIDDLETON

Snake Alley

Be sure to note how the bricks are laid narrow edge up, each a little higher than the brick above it in order to provide extra footing for the horses who hauled wagons of freight up and down the alley. Note, too, the limestone curbing and brick sidewalks in Victorian neighborhoods here and in towns throughout this Middle Mississippi River region.

MOSQUITO PARK *(4)* on 3rd & Franklin streets in the historic *North Hill* area is a small park located on a bluff overlooking the Mississippi River and a riverfront park. Locals will claim the river views here are the best for "hundreds of miles."

THE JENNIE COULTER DAY CARE CENTER (313 Washington St.) *Day Care* in a classic Victorian neighborhood? No, the sign is only commemorative--but yes, there is a story here, encompassing murder, drunken brawls among wandering "river rats," and the *Mission of Jennie Coulter.*

The Coulter house dates from early in Burlington's history, having been built from timbers used to construct the scaffold on which were hanged the notorious Hodges Brothers, found guilty of murdering a wealthy farmer.

The execution of the Hodges brothers in July 1845, was witnessed by thousands of men, women, and children, many of whom arrived by steamboat to see the spectacle. The death parade was lead by four companies of armed riflemen, followed by the prisoners in a wagon, dressed in shrouds and seated upon their coffins. A brass band followed, playing a dirge.

As macabre as it sounds today, such death parades appear, from newspaper articles, to have been well-planned and promoted spectacles of the time.

Jennie Coulter and the "Willow Patch"

For nearly 80 years, the low-lying willow patch along what is now Bluff Road, at the north end of Burlington, had been a haven for "river rats"--a term claimed affectionately today by most riverside dwellers but which then referred to vagrants who would meander the Mississippi River in "cabinboats," stopping at makeshift communities like the Willow Patch for brief intervals and then moving on. Very often, such camps sheltered not only the unemployable and the alcoholics, but also murderers, thieves, and others seeking protection from the law.

Jennie Coulter, a local social worker and missionary, was one of only a very few "decent" outsiders allowed to move safely within the colony. In the March 1920 *Gazette,* Jennie recalled her own efforts in 1916 to establish a mission and Sunday School in the Willow Patch.

"When I first went out there in the north bottoms to conduct the Mission, a colony of perhaps fifty people lived in rough cabin boats scattered here and there and connected by a network of planks. I started the Sunday School by giving a gold star to every child that did not take a drink of liquor all week long. There were few stars given out at first, but later the children would refuse to drink in order to get a star at the Mission.

"May Woods was hailed as 'Queen' of the colony. With one exception, when her man came after me with an ax, they always treated me with respect while I was conducting the Mission. "

It was reported that, "simple curiosity did much to entice residents to the little cabinboat where Jennie Coulter held

Sunday Services. All were impressed by the sincere voice of the slight little woman who could barely be heard above the lapping of waves outside."

CRAPO *(2,* pronounced CRAY-po) and DANKWARDT PARK *(1)* along the Great River Road, South Main Street, past the Port of Burlington Welcome Center.) Over 100 acres of parkland along the west bank of the Mississippi River. The Great River Road crosses *Cascade Ravine* in the park, one of many ravines which dissect the city. A paved walking path through Cascade Ravine provides convenient access to the relatively undisturbed plant and wildlife in the area.

Each of Burlington's ravines provide such abundant shelter for wildlife that one citizen described Burlington as "a game preserve masquerading as a city. "

The *Hawkeye Log Cabin* in Crapo Park overlooks the Mississippi River at the point where, in 1805, Zebulon Pike claimed the area for a government fort. This area was called *Sho-Quo-Quon* or "Flint Hills" by the Indians. As all tribes needed the flint in the early 1800s for their firearms, it was considered a neutral area. The small museum, open only Wednesday and Thursday afternoons, houses a collection of pioneer tools and furnishings.

ROCK ISLAND FREIGHT HOUSE (Front Street at the corner of High Street). Dating from 1898, this is the only remaining physical evidence in Burlington of the most important north-south rail line in Iowa. It is one of the few remaining buildings representing the train yards that once dominated the riverfront.

The CHICAGO, BURLINGTON & QUINCY RAILROAD was also significant to the development of Burlington. Charles Perkins scored a coup for the railroad when he purchased the creek bed which proved to be the only incline suitable for the line which came from Chicago and headed west in 1855. The unusually steep incline was used to test the air brake perfected by Westinghouse. Approximately 26 freight trains from the Burlington Northern line still run along the Mississippi River each day.

With river traffic carrying manufacturing products north and south, and the railroad line crossing east and west through the city, Burlington became a major center for small manufacturing, wholesale and distribution businesses.

BURLINGTON & MISSOURI RIVER RAILROAD PASSENGER STATION (237 S. Fourth, 1856). Burlington was one of four Iowa cities granted an east-west railroad charter. All the railroad companies competed in a great race to Council Bluffs on the Missouri River, from whence the Union-Pacific line lead to Utah where it joined the Central Pacific line from San Francisco.

THE APPLE TREES MUSEUM *(3)* on Dill Street is located in a remaining portion of the old Charles Perkins home. It houses Indian artifacts and many of the original Perkins furnishings. Open Wednesday and Sunday afternoon, 1:30-4:30 p.m.

Perkins moved the headquarters of the C.B. & Q. to Burlington after he and his wife (a Boston Forbes) settled at the Apple Trees. A public playground is on the site.

RIVERBOAT GAMBLING CASINO (Front and Washington streets). The *Emerald Lady* floating casino has regularly scheduled cruises between Burlington, Ft. Madison, and Keokuk. For current prices and cruise schedules call 800-322-4FUN.

THE BURLINGTON *HAWKEYE* is considered to be the oldest daily newspaper published in Iowa. James Edwards began his paper, the Fort Madison PATRIOT, in 1838. He moved it to Burlington in 1839 where his first issue began promoting the identification of Iowans as *Hawkeyes.* By the end of the year Edwards had changed the name of his paper to THE HAWKEYE AND IOWA PATRIOT.

THE IOWA "HAWKEYES"

Historians generally agree that it was a pioneer Burlington lawyer, Judge David Rorer, who deliberately promoted the nickname *Hawkeyes.* He had observed that the inhabitants of other new Midwestern states were acquiring rather unfortunate nicknames--the Illinois *Suckers* (referring to the southern leadminers who returned downriver each winter), Missouri *Pukes,* Michigan *Wolverines,* Wisconsin *Badgers,* and Minnesota *Gophers.*

It is likely he adapted the nickname *Hawkeyes* from the then-popular novels of James Fennimore Cooper *(The Last of the Mohicans and The Deerslayer)* wherein the main character, a wise and courageous woodsman, is called *Hawkeye* by admiring Indians. Rorer's home still stands at 906 N. 5th Street in Burlington.

STARKER-LEOPOLD HISTORIC DISTRICT (east end of Clay Street at the bluff.) The Starker House, c. 1870, was the boyhood home of noted American naturalist Aldo Leopold *(A Sand County Almanac).* His grandfather, Charles Starker, was a German immigrant architect and banker involved in many of the cultural improvements in Burlington, including Crapo Park. The Leopold House is the childhood home of another of Starker's grandsons, former wood duck authority Frederick Leopold.

Nearby Attractions

GEODE STATE PARK located 12 miles west of Burlington (follow *USH 34* west to Middletown, then *STH 79*). Geode display. *Geodes must not be removed from the park.* Fishing · swimming · boating · picnicking · camping

SEVEN PONDS PARK, (10 miles north of Burlington off *USH 61*). Waterslide · swimming beach · camping · fishing · a petting zoo

STARR'S CAVE Nature Center and Preserve just north of Burlington's Sunnyside Avenue and down Irish Ridge Road (about three miles) offers natural history displays, live animals for observation, and restroom facilities. Relatively undeveloped limestone cave is open to the public. Picnicking, hiking, but no camping on this 140-acre forested park.

GRANDPA BILL'S FARM, 10 miles north of Burlington off *USH 61* (near *Seven Ponds*). 100 year old farm with crafts, hayrack rides, Iowa meals and the Pepsi Country Barn Theater.

MT. PLEASANT (West of Burlington on *USH 34* at *STH 218*, 50 miles south of Iowa City). The home of *Iowa Wesleyan College,* the oldest liberal arts college west of the Mississippi (1842). Two large museums house steam tractors, engines, and other antique agricultural implements. Open mid-April to mid-October. Home of the annual *Midwest Old Thresher's Reunion,* which is considered to be one of the nation's top ten events.

GEODES

Burlington and Keokuk are in the center of a unique geologic distribution of *geodes*. Samples are available at gift shops and displayed at the Burlington Welcome Center. One visitor told of going geode hunting and returning with 200 pounds of rock in his vehicle. The geodes are generally 2 to 4 inches round and can be found in rock bars in creeks and embedded in shale outcroppings. Rock hammers, chisels, etc. are required to extract them from rock.

Two types of Geode are found in the area. The Warsaw type, found south of Keokuk, is smoother and contains calcite crystals. The Keokuk type is generally found north of Keokuk, has a rougher shell, and contains quartz crystals. The crystals form when a mud ball is trapped within the sedimentary deposits which eventually form limestone. As the mud dissolves away, minerals slowly leach through the limestone and reform as crystals within the cavity.

The excitement in opening a geode lies in beholding for the first time what has taken nature 250 million years to create. To open a geode, wrap string around the geode several times--soak the string with fuel oil, set it afire, and after the fire goes out, drop the geode in a pail of cold water. Remove the geode from the water and tap the shell along the string line.

A book, *THE FABULOUS KEOKUK GEODES* by Stephen R. Sinotte, contains further information, pictures and maps.

USH 61 is the most convenient way to leave Burlington, but it doesn't matter which side of the river the traveler follows to Fort Madison. However, one will want to cross to the Illinois side from Ft. Madison to the south.

Iowa's Great River Road follows CTH X62. Numerous old buildings made from native limestone line this route. A llama farm makes an interesting stop for youngsters as does the recreation area on the Skunk River.

SKUNK RIVER RECREATION AREA offers a tiny camping area (some electric hookups), boat access, and playground.

8 Miles to Fort Madison, Iowa

Crystals inside Geode

Special Events

Snake Alley Criterium, Burlington, (last weekend in May). Olympic-style bike racing. Top amateur cyclists from all over the world race up Snake Alley as many as twenty times!

Burlington Steamboat Days (mid-June). National rock, pop, country, jazz, and other groups perform daily at outdoor stage, the Memorial Auditorium, and the Port of Burlington Building. Fireworks, parades, carnival, food and beverages.

MADRAC, Annual Canoe Trip along the Iowa shore averages about 25 miles per day. Open to the public. Headquarters are located in Burlington. Also organizers of *International Dragon Boat Racing* teams. For further information, call (319) 752-4142.

Burlington Heritage Fest (Labor Day Weekend) salutes Burlington's multi-ethnic heritage. Entertainment, food, old-time demonstrations. Extensive window displays of Burlington history.

Mt. Pleasant, *Annual Thresher's Reunion* (five days, ending Labor Day weekend) is considered to be one of the top events in America. America's largest steam show, authentic threshing days demonstrations, music, Buckskinner camp, narrow gauge train with several steam locomotives. Campground on site.

A Brief History of Des Moines County

The name Des Moines first appears in the writings of a French traveler who indicates that in 1699 he and explorer Pierre Charles Le Suer called the river *". . .la Riveriere des Moingona after the Moingona Indian tribe dwelling along its banks."*

French fur traders Radisson and Groseillers, too, wrote of the Moingona Indians and the great forked river which terminated in the Gulf. A later French writer, Father Pierre Charlevoix, wrote, *"The river Moingona issues from an immense meadow, which swarms with Buffaloes and other wild beasts: at its entrance to the Mississippi, it is very shallow and narrow."* Buffalo frequented the Iowa prairies only during western droughts. They no longer appeared after about 1815.

Eventually the French name *Des Moines* meaning *of the Moines* was applied not only to the river and this county, but also to the capital city of Iowa.

Burlington was first settled in 1833 and served as the temporary capital city of the Wisconsin Territory from 1837 to 1838--a plum granted to the Des Moines County representatives who then provided the majority vote moving the territorial capital permanently to the current Wisconsin capital city of Madison. From 1838 to 1840, Burlington was the first capital city of the newly formed *Iowa Territory*. By 1856, 15,000 residents lived in Burlington. Another 20,000 pioneers crossed the ferry from Illinois to settle the western prairies.

LEE COUNTY

Fort Madison and Keokuk, Iowa

Lee County represents the oldest of the Spanish Land Grants made to French-Canadians along the Iowa shore. These Canadians were ambitious traders who in turn promised to keep the peace among Indians and to promote loyalty to Spain. Louis Honore Tesson received this particular grant of 6,000 acres at the head of the Des Moines Rapids in 1799 and established a settlement near Montrose, IA. A large land grant was also made to Basil Girard near McGregor, Iowa. Julien Dubuque acquired the Spanish Lead Mines. *(See map, Burlington to Keokuk, p. 167.)*

The county was established by the First Wisconsin Territorial Legislature and named for Robert E. Lee, then a young army Lieutenant who, in 1836, conducted a survey of the Des Moines (or *Lower)* Rapids for the U.S. War Department.

Fort Madison, Iowa
Population 11,618

Upon approaching Fort Madison from Burlington on *USH 61*, there is a significant dip from the ridge down to the riverfront. Many of the river towns were established in such ravines as they provided protection from winter winds and the most convenient paths inland.

Fort Madison was incorporated in 1837 as Madison City, named for its early frontier fort, which was named in turn for then-President James Madison. Early on it thrived as a center for grain milling and distilling, pork packing and saw milling. Its longtime rival on the river is Keokuk, its twin city to the south. To this day, Lee County is the only Iowa county with two county seats--South Lee County offices are in Keokuk, North Lee County in Fort Madison. The *County Courthouse* in Fort Madison dates from 1841 and is the oldest continuously used courthouse in Iowa.

Today there are numerous small manufacturing companies in town which take advantage of the convenient river and rail transportation. Sheaffer Pen, which originated in Fort Madison, has its large plant along the riverfront. Recent excavations revealed the original fort foundations in the vicinity of the Shaeffer-Eaton parking lot at a depth of about nine feet.

Dial Corporation employs over 700 people at its plant which supplies all *Armour* and *Armour Star* meat products distributed west of the Mississippi. It is the largest meat packing plant in the world.

Of special interest to the visitor will be the replica of *Old Fort Madison* in Riverview Park, the nearby Lee County Historic Center at the old *Santa Fe Depot,* and Fort Madison's historic architecture dating from the mid-19th century. The *Emerald Lady* floating casino docks just west of the Old Fort.

A granddaughter of Betsy Ross built a home in town at 716-720 Avenue ''F'' which is on the National Historic Register. There is a beautiful square with Victorian houses on 9th Street, in the ''F'' and ''G'' area. Fort Madison's streets are numbered 1st to 48th from the bridge west and from Avenue "R" to "A" from the river's edge to the north. The river flows northeast to southwest. A city map and guided auto tour are available at the Visitor Center on *USH 61*.

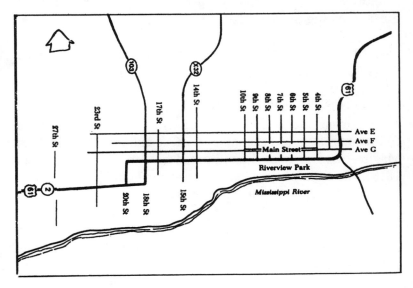

City of Fort Madison, IA

THE IOWA STATE PENITENTIARY rises abruptly as *USH 61* curves down into Fort Madison. Large blocks of pitted limestone and decorative stone turrets surround the walls of the old portion of the prison. Built in the 1839 with prison labor, this is the oldest prison west of the Mississippi River. It was a territorial prison before Iowa became a state.

THE FORT MADISON VISITOR CENTER, built to resemble a blockhouse from the old fort, is located riverside of the prison, just before the toll bridge into Illinois. An historical time-line for Old Fort Madison outside the center provides a quick, clear orientation to significant local history.

THE SANTA FE BRIDGE to Illinois has, at 525 feet, the longest double-decked, *swingspan bridge* in the world. Automobiles cross on the upper deck of the 3,347-foot long bridge while trains use the lower deck. The span swings open to allow the barges through. Barges have precedence over train traffic crossing the Mississippi River.

SMALL BOAT HARBOR (east end of Riverview Park, near the Santa Fe Bridge). Courtesy slips · fuel · small store · repair shop

THE LONE CHIMNEY MONUMENT *(USH 61* and 4th Street across from the Shaeffer building). Erected in 1908 to commemorate several chimneys left standing after Old Fort Madison was evacuated and burned by American soldiers in 1813. The Chimney, which had been randomly placed is now known to be at the original site of Blockhouse 1.

RIVERVIEW PARK is comprised of 40 acres along the city's riverfront. The Old Fort Madison replica is located on the grounds, as is a marina, and riverboat dock.

OLD FORT MADISON REPLICA (located in Riverview Park and Open late May to mid-September). The replica of Old Fort Madison (1808-1813) was built to scale by inmates at the Iowa State Penitentiary, disassembled, and rebuilt at its current site.

Lois Koch

The visitor's first reaction might be *it's so small!* In fact, except for the unusual "tail," this was a fairly typical size and layout for the forts guarding the frontiers at this time.

By 1808, Fort Dearborn (Chicago) and Fort Detroit (Michigan) along with Fort Madison (the first on the upper Mississippi River) each housed somewhere between 30 and 90 soldiers, officers and officer families. Privates earned perhaps $5/month.

The frontier forts served mainly to protect the associated *fur factory* or trading posts where the Indians traded furs, lead, and hides for such manufactured goods as knives, traps, blankets, fish hooks and whiskey. Many Indians had developed strong economic and cultural ties with the British and French during a century of fur trading in the river valley. Determined to maintain this relationship, the British actively encouraged a deep-seated distrust of the Americans.

Burning and Evacuation of Old Fort Madison in 1813
St. Louis *Globe-Democrate, March 1902*

In 1813, the deaths of six soldiers by Indian ambush in a one-week period precipitated the evacuation of the fort. A trench was dug to the river during the night and the garrison managed to crawl out with their boats and personal belongings before the Indians became aware of the evacuation. The last man out set fire to the fort and the troops escaped down river toward St. Louis. Of the three frontier garrisons, Fort Madison, had survived local Indian pressure longer than either of the others.

Much of the limestone foundation found in the replica was recovered from the original fort site and the reddish burn marks from the fire are still visible.

SANTA FE DEPOT HISTORIC CENTER (just west and north of Riverside Park). The depot was built in 1910 as the Santa Fe Depot and is now operated by the North Lee County Historical Society. Open May through September. Exhibits include artifacts (buttons, china, ironworks) recovered from the excavations of Old Fort Madison as well as displays of early pioneer life in the area.

The Santa Fe Railroad

The Santa Fe Railroad began in Atchison but was soon moved to Kansas City. Fort Madison/Keokuk marked the half-way point between Chicago and Kansas City. The decision was made to bring the train up through Keokuk and to cross the river at Fort Madison. As the northernmost stop on the Santa Fe Line, Fort Madison became the main railroad hub. Called "Shopton" by the railroad industry, over 1,000 people were employed in the shops repairing and refurbishing railroad cars.

SPECIAL EVENTS

Civil War Reenactment, Late April, Keokuk. Visitors are welcome at this authentic encampment. Reenactment of the *Battle of Pea Ridge.* Costumed Military Ball and other related activities.

Rendezvous! Memorial Day Weekend, Old Fort Madison. Buckskinner camp, competitions.

Riverfest, 4th July week, Ft. Madison. Nationally known entertainment, carnival in Riverview Park.

Art in the Park, Mid-August, Ft. Madison. Area artists dsplay and sell their work in Central Park.

Rendezvous! Early September, Old Fort Madison. Buckskinner camp, competitions.

Tri-State Rodeo. Weekend after Labor Day, Fort Madison, Nationally known 3-day rodeo. Wild bucking horses, brahma bulls, and other rodeo competitions.

The law required livestock shipped from the west to be unloaded from the train cars every three days for a three day rest. Fort Madison was just such a rest stop for the cattle, wild horses, and brahma bulls being shipped east from Colorado and Montana to Chicago. Thus the start, in 1937-38, of a three-day rodeo intended to exercise the animals and help the cowboys kill time.

Bald Eagle Appreciation Days, mid-January, Keokuk. Hourly seminars, exhibits, lectures, observation areas with spotting scopes and naturalists on duty. Free shuttles to all events and the riverfront. Free Admission.

From Ft. Madison, travelers will want to cross the swing span bridge to Niota, Illinois and visit the restored Mormon city of **Nauvoo** *(see Chapter 11, page 155, Hancock County). Return to Keokuk, IA, on USH 136 west at Hamilton, IL.*

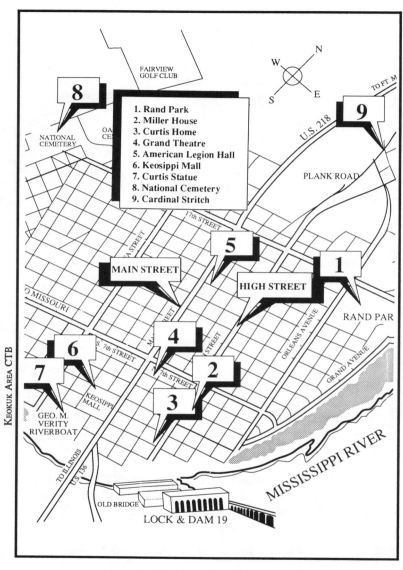

1. Rand Park
2. Miller House
3. Curtis Home
4. Grand Theatre
5. American Legion Hall
6. Keosippi Mall
7. Curtis Statue
8. National Cemetery
9. Cardinal Stritch

Keokuk, Iowa, City Map

Keokuk, Iowa
Population 12,451

Keokuk has been endowed with entire neighborhoods of beautiful 19th century buildings. A self-guided walking tour brochure is available at the Tourism Office, 401 Main, and at local motels and restaurants.

Keokuk also claims one of the largest wintering populations of bald eagles on the Mississippi River. If you are visiting between November and March check out the open water below the dam in the early morning. During the annual Bald Eagle Appreciation days in mid-January, manned observation points are set up along the riverfront to help observers. Please note that wintering eagles and other waterfowl are easily stressed by human contact. Stay in or near your car. Do NOT try to approach or harass eagles.

Things to See in Keokuk

MILLER HOUSE MUSEUM (318 North 5th Street, Thursday -Sunday, 1 to 4 p.m.) is operated by the Lee County Historical Society at the former home of Justice Samuel Miller. It is an excellent display of local and area history. Miller was a Kentucky lawyer who eventually became an Iowa Republican and was appointed by President Abraham Lincoln to the U.S. Supreme Court.

ST. JOHN'S EPISCOPAL CHURCH, at Fourth & Concert streets, boasts two Tiffany stained glass windows. One is a grey angel about halfway down the west wall, the other a brown angel in the southwest corner. Note the milky texture of the glass which was distinctive of the Tiffany style. The ceiling of the church is also notable--it is built to resemble the upside down keel of a ship. Ask for brochure at the church office.

RAND PARK is an extensive city park overlooking the Mississippi River. It is located at the foot of Grand Avenue which is graced by a parade of magnificent blufftop homes. The park has formal flower gardens and a bronze statue dedicated to the memory of Keokuk (though the statue of a Sioux plains Indian bears no relationship to the appearance of the respected Sac warrior). In addition to Keokuk, neighboring counties of Wapello, Tama, Mahaska, Poweshiek, and Appanoose also commemorate local Native American leaders.

Keokuk, for whom this city is named, shared leadership of the area Sac/Mesquakie tribes with his rival, Black Hawk. Keokuk's father was half French, his mother a true Sac. Any historical mention of dealings with Keokuk includes comments attesting to his eloquence, wisdom, and fine sense of honor.

The city's name also recalls the fact that the area was established as a Sac/Mesquakie half-breed reservation in January 1825. The legal entanglements later involved in allotting individual Indians ownership of 60 acre tracts in this former "Half-Breed Tract" provided steady employment for as many as 60 lawyers who flooded Fort Madison and Keokuk in the mid-1800s.

GEORGE M. VERITY RIVERBOAT MUSEUM (Victory Park, on the riverfront). 9-5 p.m. Small entrance fee. Now a museum of upper Mississippi River commercial shipping history, the drydocked *George M. Verity* was the first of four new riverboats built in 1927 by the U.S. Government to revive barge transportation on the Mississippi. As the *S.S. Thorpe,* it moved barges from St. Louis to St. Paul.

OBSERVATION DECK. The old Hamilton-Keokuk swingspan bridge provides an overlook of the river and Lock and Dam 19. Picnic tables and benches.

LOCK & DAM 19 Here at Keokuk is the highest "step" in the stairway of locks & dams that were created to make the Mississippi navigable for commercial vessels. The 38-foot lift is necessary to provide clearance over the rocky rapids formed by glacial debris. The pool behind it is the largest of the pools created by the dams. The lock is 1200 feet long--large enough to handle the full length of a fleet of barges. This is the only dam besides Lock and Dam 1 which is used to produce electricity.

MISSISSIPPI POOL 19, also known as LAKE COOPER, is Iowa's largest "lake." 30,000 acres and 240 miles of shoreline. Bass fishing · sailing · boating · skiing and scenery

A Brief History of the Union Electric Power Plant and Dam

The Keokuk Dam was built by Chief Engineer Hugh L. Cooper for Union Electric between 1910 and 1913. Cooper was hired for this job in January of 1910 after he had designed the hydro-electric plant at Niagara Falls. Having completed the dam in Keokuk, he left for a project in Russia which effectively took the rest of his life to complete. Cooper is honored with a bronze plaque on the city's river front.

The giant dam and electrical plant was begun in Hamilton, IL. 119 gates were put up, eight gates at a time. 2,500 immigrants were brought in, many from Sweden, to do 12-hour shifts of hard labor. 1.3 million cubic yards of earth and rock were excavated. 565,000 cubic yards of concrete were brought in from Portland/Atlas plants to complete the dam which is 7/8 mile long.

Chief Engineer Cooper developed much of the technology and equipment necessary to complete the project which required 2-1/2 years and 25 million dollars to build. Pictures recording the building of the dam are displayed at the Samuel Miller Museum.

MARK TWAIN CENTER at the Keokuk Public Library (210 North 5th Street) contains a collection of some of his works and personal belongings.

Like Muscatine, Keokuk was an early, brief home of Samuel Clemens. His brother, Orion Clemens, operated a printing office on Main Street in town and married Mollie Stotts, a Keokuk woman. Orion urged Sam to stay in Keokuk to help run the printing office in 1855.

The *Keokuk Post* purchased Sam's first published articles, a series of farcical travel tales called *"The Snodgrass Letters."* He was paid $5 each. By late 1856 Clemens left Keokuk and served as a pilot's apprentice and pilot between 1857 and 1861.

It was after his stint as river pilot that Sam took the name *Mark Twain.* In 1889 he bought a house in Keokuk for his mother, Jane Clemens. Located at 626 High Street, the home is still a private residence.

STEAMBOAT CASINO CRUISES (711 Mississippi Drive). Keokuk is the home port and winter dock for the *Emerald Lady* floating casino. Expect excellent meals, entertainment and scenery. $200 loss limit on all Iowa gambling boats. Prices for the cruises may vary from $8 to $38 depending on the cruise, time of year, and which meals are involved. Call 800-322-4FUN. For details on the Bus Express from Milwaukee, St. Louis, Des Moines, Hannibal and other midwestern towns, call 800-4BUS-FUN

A Brief History of Keokuk

The town of Keokuk introduced itself into history in 1829 as a small landing at the foot of the Des Moines Rapids (or "Lower" rapids while those near Rock Island are the "Upper" rapids). This same year, the first railroad operations in the U.S. began in eastern Pennsylvania and Maryland, though it would be 25 years before a railroad reached Keokuk.

Sometimes called "Stillwell's Landing," this first permanent white settlement west of the Mississippi River and north of the state of Missouri provided a wood yard for refueling the steamboats which were transporting supplies to fortune seekers and fur trappers making their way to the Galena lead mines. A small fleet of keelboats was held here for "lightering" freight over the rapids when the water was too low for steamboats to pass over. Thus the nickname *Gate City* was early applied to the town.

In 1819, Caleb Atwater described the village in his diary, *"The village is a small one, containing twenty families perhaps. The American Fur Company have a store here, and there is a tavern. Many Indians were fishing, and their lights on the rapids, in a dark night, were darting about, appearing and disappearing like so many fire flies; the constant roaring of the water on the rapids, the occasional Indian yell, the lights of their fires on the shore, and the boisterous mirth of the people at the doggery (tavern) attracted my attention occasionally, while we were lying here. Fish were caught in abundance.... The beach on the western shore is narrow, and the hills of moderate elevation, come quite down to the high water mark. Large blocks of coarse sandstone have been floated down, on the ice at different times, from the St. Peters [Minnesota] River, and lodged on the beach. The rocks in place are limestone though great numbers of geodes of quartz cover the beach."*

In 1841, the population was estimated at only 150 people. Thirteen years later the population had multiplied to 5,044. The cooper's daughter became the wife of George H. Williams, the U.S. Attorney General during the last years of President Grant's administration.

Keokuk and the Civil War

U.S. NATIONAL CEMETERY, 1701 "J" Street. Keokuk, the site of a major military hospital, was Iowa's link to the Civil War. Unfortunately, many of the wounded transported up the Mississippi from southern battlefields were eventually buried in Keokuk. The National Cemetery in Keokuk is one of 12 originally designated by the U.S. Congress. It was the first to be located west of the Mississippi and the only National Cemetery in Iowa.

As the state's southernmost city, Keokuk became the embarkation point for over 80,000 soldiers mustered into the Union forces. Keokuk's fledgling "medical college" formed the core of what eventually became a government hospital encompassing seven buildings. It eventually migrated to become the Medical School at the University of Iowa in Iowa City.

The Battle of Pea Ridge, Arkansas, which is reenacted each April, was led by Major General Samuel Curtis--former mayor of Keokuk, a West Point trained civil engineer, lawyer, and Congressman. The Union victory at Pea Ridge pushed Confederate forces out of Missouri, saving Missouri and the Missouri River for the Union. Curtis was then appointed to oversee the development of the Union Pacific railroad to the Pacific. A large portrait of Curtis hangs in Omaha, NE, to honor that effort.

Annie Wittenmeyer

Annie Wittenmeyer was a Keokuk citizen who became nationally known for her war efforts. In the 1850s, Annie established a school at the local Poor House. Her interest in "her boys" who went to war led to the organization of the "Iowa Sanitary Commission," which sent first-aid supplies to the Union battlefields.

Annie also personally lobbied President Lincoln for better nutrition for convalescent soldiers and was issued special orders in 1864 allowing her and her ladies to operate special diet kitchens. She established America's first *Soldiers' Orphans' Homes* to fulfill promises made to dying soldiers.

Wittenmeyer was allowed to pass through all lines at all times. U.S. Grant said of Wittenmeyer, *"No soldier on the firing line gave more heroic service than she rendered."*

BASIL WILLIAMS

Civil War reenactments and buckskinner camps provide visitor and reenacters alike an opportunity to relive significant eras in America's varied, dramatic history.

Area Campgrounds

Sugar Valley Campground (Rt. 2, Box 200, *USH 61 & 218)* Open year round. Pool · rec room · Laundry

Wally World (.5 mile off *USH 61*, Ft. Madison). Swimming·fishing · restaurant · Mini Golf.

Rodeo Park, Ft. Madison. Electrical hookups

City of Keokuk (Riverfront/Victory Park). Electrical hookups

Hickory Haven Campground (RR 2, Box 68, Keokuk). Open year round. Hiking trails · stocked pond · swimming pool · hookups

Captain Milford Lawrence has spent 44 years on the river. He is a Licensed Master *and* Licensed First Class Pilot *for the Illinois, Ohio, Tennessee, Cumberland, Upper, and Lower Mississippi rivers.*

INSIGHT

Captain Milford Lawrence
Riverboat Pilot

"There are no two rivers that are alike. The piloting is unique to each, as is the scenery and the history. This is purely the Mississippi River. It doesn't compare in any way to any other river.

*"The people living ashore are so interesting. They love their river, their boats, the fish, the recreation. They feel so much ownership of the river and its valleys. Those of us who work on the river feel this appreciation, too; a strong sense that this river belongs to **all** of us. We have to make room for one another and all our varied interests. It's vital to protect this river, its wildlife.*

"I think its hard for people to even imagine the vast importance of the river in the lives of millions of people in this great nation, and all those foreign countries that depend on our foreign trade. Electric plants, drinking water, heat, and grain are supplied by or moved upon this river.

"Mark Twain would be astonished at the power, the scope of river traffic today when compared to the paddlewheelers that ran the river in his day. The sheer power of the diesel towboats, the steel hulls that have replaced the wooden hulls. The steamboat pilots really were the pioneers of river transportation as we know it today.

"I've seen the Locks on the upper river put in. I've seen the corn business explode because of the navigational technol-

ogy that allows us to **move** *the corn. Improvements in agriculture and shipping have developed hand-in-hand. One barge with a 9-foot draft can move 1500 tons of corn. The freight pushed by a single towboat and its crew of 11 men is worth many millions of dollars and takes the place of 20 train engineers, 20 firemen, 20 brakemen, etc. If something should happen to the lock system, it would cripple the American economy. Trucks and trains or airplanes could not possibly make up the difference.*

"The main thing a Midwestern farmer thinks about is getting his harvest of grain to the elevator. But that's just the beginning. There is more corn produced in the upper Midwest than anywhere else in the world. More grain is moved on the Mississippi than on any other river system. The sight of ocean-going barges from around the world picking up Midwestern grain in New Orleans is sobering. Few farmers begin to realize the number of people world-wide that are fed by Midwestern corn.

"The Indians called this the "Father of Waters" and that's exactly what it is today. I'm a long-run pilot. I just know what I see on the river."

HANCOCK COUNTY

Nauvoo, Illinois

> **Fort Madison to Nauvoo along *STH 96***
> **Dallas City, IL, 6 miles**
> **Quincy, IL, 45 miles**
> **Hannibal, MO, 65 miles**

Of all the miles along the Great River Road, no stretch encompasses so well the vigor, lusts, and dreams of the 19th century American west as do stately, politic Quincy, IL, the childlike exuberance of Hannibal, MO, or the spiritual fervor of the Mormons who left Nauvoo, IL, enmass to colonize the far reaches of the continent. *(Area map, p. 167)*

Nauvoo is the most extensive restoration project in the Midwest and visitors should plan to spend no less than 1/2 day in the restored city of Nauvoo. However, the tiny towns of Pontoosuc, Niota, and Dallas City on Illinois' *STH 96 north* just after crossing the river at Fort Madison are untouristed little river towns well worth a visit for architectural and cultural interest. As you travel, watch for simple 150-year old stone homes, sometimes derelict, often in the process of restoration. Many beautiful restored stone mansions still preside over the quiet villages.

Pontoosuc, Illinois
Population 264

There would be little argument that Pontoosuc's (Pon-TOO-Sic) best days have passed. The lock & dam system drowned the better part of the riverfront commercial district more than 50 years ago. Where once a whole town thrived on commercial fishing and related businesses, today there is only one resident fisherman.

Here and there simple native stone buildings stare blankly, still owned by "an old family." The fisherman cleaning his nets is happy to display his catch in an old livestock tank. There is a park of sorts south of town and along the river. A creek marks the site of an early mill. A dike of sandbags still surrounds a house.

"My dad refused to take the sandbags down after the last flood," his daughter tells me. *"He's fishing now, though he'd love to talk. I remember when we traded fish for vegetables and milk from the farmers. We all had to work at the fishing and do the route. Farmers came to our doors, too. It seems in those days the market came to the people."*

Her mother's face is brown, lean, weathered. She remembers how often the river has flooded the town. *"My friend, a Mexican woman, used to call the river mean. One day we can walk along it and it's just real pretty. Then it turns mean, and mucks up the house, or drowns a child."*

For this family, Pontoosuc's glory days really erupted nearly 150 years ago, when it was the Pontoosucan militia, *"The Bloody Pontoosucans,"* who stood up to the "marauding" Mormons during the *Mormon Wars* with their neighbors in Nauvoo.

THE 1850s GUEST HOUSE B&B, a colonial Greek Revival home along side *STH 96* is the finest house in Pontoosuc. The proprietor is an historian at heart and only too happy to share with guests her interest in the architecture and history of the Guest House. It has massively thick stone walls and strange hollows beneath the basement floor which may well date from the days of the Underground Railroad. Home tours by appointment. Gift Shop.

Dallas City, Illinois
Population 1,800

Founded in 1859, there are several large Victorian homes, many of native limestone, including a stone Richardsonian-style residence south of the supper club. The Walker Fish/ Fur Market sells fresh fish, oysters and other seafood, and trapping supplies. Camping, public boat docks, marina, cafes, and motel are all available.

RIVERFRONT HISTORICAL MARKER   Bronze plaque on a granite boulder notes that Lincoln spoke here October 12, 1858, as part of the Lincoln/Douglas Senate debates. The traveler may note that granite boulders are not normally found in the driftless area north of Burlington. Such boulders and other orphan rocks are deposited by glacial movements in the area.

U.S. FISH AND WILDLIFE SERVICE

Commercial fishermen bring in the morning's catch.

Nauvoo, Illinois
Population 1,100

Nauvoo is a Hebrew word meaning "beautiful" or "pleasant place." Plan to spend no less than 1/2 day here, though it would be easy to spend much more time, and take in an evening meal at the old *Hotel Nauvoo*. All tours and activities within the restored city of Nauvoo are free.

THE UPTOWN INFORMATION CENTER is located across the street from the Hotel Nauvoo. There are many unique shops, boutiques, and antique stores in Uptown Nauvoo. The rural countryside is beautiful and the drive of two miles to the historic cemetery on East Parley Street is pleasant. Ask for the auto tour cassette tape.

THE OLD NAUVOO HOTEL (c. 1840) is well-known for excellent food and now offers overnight accommodation. The giant buffet seems self-regenerating. Open April to November. There are other popular B&Bs in the area, including *Mississippi Dreaming* which directly overlooks the Mississippi River on *STH 96* south. Check at the Information Center for updated lists.

ICARIAN LIVING HISTORY MUSEUM (Located in the restored 1846 *Mix House* on East Parley behind Nauvoo State Park). Open 2 to 5 p.m., April through November. Museum devoted to French and Icarian culture in America. Artifacts from 1849 to 1860.

After the 1846 exodus of the Mormons from Nauvoo, the *Icarians,* a communal group lead by Etienne Cabet, moved into the town in 1849. The Icarian community was short-lived. Although they also established communities in Corning, IA, St. Louis, and California, by 1898 the group had disintegrated.

Today we still enjoy *Rhubarb pie* which was introduced by the Icarians. An Icarian architect, A.J. Piquenard, designed both the Illinois and Iowa state capital buildings.

Many of the Icarians were French nationals who began the cultivation of grapes in Nauvoo. The historic *Baxter Vineyards* is one of the last remnants of the wine making industry for which Nauvoo became famous. The great, great-grandfather of the present owner was Emile Baxter who arrived to join the Icarians in 1855. His vineyard was planted in 1858 and he remained in Nauvoo when the Icarians disbanded. It is the oldest winery in Illinois.

NAUVOO STATE PARK is directly across *STH 96* from the Mormon restoration project. 148 acres, 2-1/2 miles of trails. Fishing · playground · picnicking · camping

THE NAUVOO MUSEUM is in the state park adjacent to the vineyard. Artifacts of Indians, white settlers, and Mormons are displayed in the *Rheinberger House* where one of Nauvoo's first wine cellar was located. Open May-October 1-5 p.m. Free.

A small portion of an original vineyard has been preserved at the *Nauvoo State Park Historical Museum* site. The thick, gnarled vines speak eloquently of the passage of time. The award- winning blue cheese of Nauvoo is aged in many of the old wine cellars of Nauvoo.

NAUVOO RESTORATION, INC

Composite sketch of the restored buildings of old Nauvoo.

THE RESTORED CITY OF OLD NAUVOO. Many Mormon homes and businesses have been restored, including those of Joseph and Emma Smith and Brigham Young. Guides provide information at each building. Many buildings, including the home of gunsmith Jonathan Browning and the *Times and Seasons* print shop, contain living museums with skilled artisans demonstrating period crafts and skills.

Both major bodies of the Mormon Church have visitor centers in the historic restored village of Nauvoo. The *R.L.D.S. (Reorganized Church of Jesus Christ of Latter Day Saints)* operates the Joseph Smith Historic Center located along *STH 96* on Water Street. Information is available here for the home and other properties of Joseph and Emma Smith.

The *L.D.S.* or main body *(The Church of Jesus Christ of Latter-day Saints)* has a vast Visitor Center on Young and Partridge streets. Visitor guides and other information are available here from 8 a.m. to 8 p.m. between Memorial Day and Labor Day, and 8:30 a.m. to 5:00 p.m. during the rest of the year.

THE TEMPLE SITE is located on the highest hill in Nauvoo. Begun in 1841, it was finished in 1846 at a cost of almost one million dollars. By that time, most of the Mormons had left Nauvoo for the Great Salt Lake Basin. It was the largest building north of St. Louis and west of Cincinnati.

Ravaged by arson in 1848, tornado, and neglect, much of the white stone from the Temple was cannibalized and may be seen in other structures in Uptown Nauvoo. A sunstone from one of the pillars is displayed on the grounds of Nauvoo State Park. Another is at the Smithsonian Institution's National Museum of American History in Washington, D.C.

THE STATUE GARDENS located at the L.D.S. visitor center should not be missed. There is something very moving in this tender tribute to the role of pioneer women and mothers. The life-sized bronze statues have eloquently captured the various stages and contributions women make throughout the course of their lives. Paid for by Mormon women, it is believed to be the largest commission in the world dedicated to women.

The life-long contributions of women are honored in the Statue Gardens behind the L.D.S. visitor center.

A Brief History of Nauvoo

The history of Nauvoo begins with the birth of Joseph Smith in 1805. While living in Palmyra, NY, Smith discovered the Golden Plates near Manchester, NY, in 1823. The Church of Jesus Christ of Latter-day Saints (Mormons) was organized in Manchester in 1830. By 1833 Joseph had moved his headquarters to Missouri, where the Mormons settled first at Independence, then several new towns in northern counties.

During the winter of 1838-39 the people of Quincy, IL, then a town of 1,600, sheltered Joseph Smith and 6,000 of his Mormon followers who were fleeing an extermination order from the governor of Missouri. That spring of 1839 the group moved to the swampy lowland of undeveloped Commerce, IL (so muddy that ''oxen became mired trying to pull the plow.''). Commerce was renamed Nauvoo and by 1845 it was only slightly smaller than Chicago (and the nation's 10th largest city) with an area population numbering almost 20,000 souls.

In 1844 Joseph Smith and his brother Hyrum were killed by a mob at the jail in Carthage, IL.

It is hardly an exaggeration to suggest that the Mormons left Illinois for the Great Salt Lake Basin partially to avoid civil war with their neighbors. What caused such ill feelings or the breaking of ranks by the Mormons themselves is a little more difficult to understand.

One key to understanding, however, was the sheer political clout wielded by this huge, like-minded voting block suddenly dropped in among the scattered townships that then existed in western Illinois. When the first Mormons crossed into Quincy from Missouri, they were welcomed and sheltered-- even though they already numbered five times the population of that significant river town.

As their numbers in Hancock County grew steadily toward 20,000, they could promise election to any politician willing to cater to them. And cater they did! Politicians literally fell all over the community, granting Nauvoo total autonomy so long as the Mormans did not break any state or federal laws. Thus Nauvoo had its own militia, its own court system, its own law enforcement, and its own education system.

It was intimidating, to say the least, to their struggling, outnumbered neighbors. Any conflict with a Mormon had to be settled in the Mormon court as did any claims by Mormons against a neighboring Gentile. Retaliatory murder, hostage-taking, and theft between Mormon and Gentile became the rule as faith in even-handed law enforcement failed.

By 1844, discontent with Joseph Smith's consolidation of power and the introduction of polygamy began to affect even the Mormon community. The split was epitomized by the opposition press established in Nauvoo itself. Before the second paper was printed, Nauvoo's city council had declared the paper a nuisance and the press was demolished. The publishers of *THE EXPOSITOR* were ejected from the Church.

Smith and the entire city council were charged by *THE EXPOSITOR* with inciting a riot. He and his brother were arrested and incarcerated at the stone county jail in Carthage on June 25, 1844. Two days later, they were attacked and killed by a mob while in the care of the State of Illinois.

No doubt, there was great concern that the Smith murders would send the huge Mormon population into a vindictive rampage, but that never happened. Tensions continued to escalate, however, with attacks against scattered Mormon towns and farms. Ultimately, the Mormons were promised protection provided they prepared to leave Illinois.

During the winter of 1845-46, intense preparations were made to move the Mormon community west of the Mississippi River. All dwellings, including the Temple, were transformed into workshops. By spring, thousands of wagons had been built and supplied.

Relations with neighboring Gentiles, had by then become so acrimonious that it was decided that an immediate exodus was necessary. In February of 1846, Brigham Young, then president of the church's governing body, directed the greatest, most successful mass exodus in American history.

Not all Mormons followed Young's contingent, however. Several groups dispersed elsewhere. Emma Smith and her group stayed along the Mississippi in Wisconsin, Iowa and Illinois and eventually formed the Reorganized Church of Jesus Christ of Latter Day Saints.

THE MORMON TRAIL

The departure of the first several thousand Mormons across the Mississippi River to Montrose, Iowa, is often equated with the Red Sea crossing in the Biblical Exodus story. The first wagons were sent on rafts amid floating ice. Before everyone had crossed, however, the ice froze solid and many Mormons walked or rode across.

The Mormons spread out for 1,400 miles, from Council Bluffs, IA, (avoiding Missouri) to the Great Salt Lake Basin. Now officially designated as the *Mormon Pioneer Trail,* this National Historic Trail with 73 historic sites is maintained by the National Park Service. It begins in Nauvoo and terminates at *Pioneer Trail State Park* in Salt Lake City, Utah.

Mormons at the front planted crops and constructed shelters for those who followed. When money for funding the exodus ran low, the last three thousand families were issued pushcarts instead of wagons. Each family physically pushed 500 pounds of belongings across the western plains.

The last groups found supply stations stripped and, as winter set in, many simply froze to death along the route. Upon arriving in the Great Basin, further difficulties met the immigrants. The arid land could not support crops so technologies learned when draining Nauvoo were reversed to provide water for irrigation. Entire herds of cattle froze to death in sudden blizzards. Insects devoured crops.

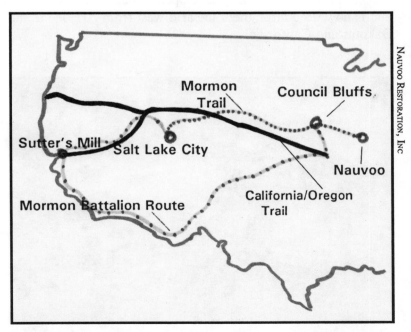

Map of the Mormon Trail. More settlers moved west across the Mormon Trail than across either the California or Oregon trails. Even the numbers who moved to California during the Gold Rush Days did not equal the number of Mormons who moved to the Great Salt Lake Basin.

Along the way, 500 men were mustered into the Mexican War. They then participated in the California Gold Rush at Sutter's Mill before rejoining their brethren in the Great Salt Lake Basin. During Brigham Young's administration as the 2nd President of the Church of Latter-day Saints, over 70,000 people from the U.S.A., Europe, and Canada settled in Utah. Three hundred cities and towns were established.

The Mormons literally had moved Nauvoo 1,000 miles past the limits of civilization at that time. The skilled tradesmen, craftsmen, artists, and professionals provided a way-station in the middle of the wilderness which enabled many other immigrants to reach the west coast who might not otherwise have succeeded. Brigham Young developed a doctrine for water use that is now used throughout the arid west from Arizona to the Dakotas and California.

Departing from Nauvoo, portion of a mural painted by Lynn Fausett.
Displayed at Pioneer Trails State Park, Salt Lake City, Utah.

In 1950, a statue of Brigham Young was placed in the *American Hall of Fame* in the Rotunda of the Capitol in Washington, D.C. where Young was honored as *the great colonizer.*

THE CARTHAGE JAIL on *USH 136* east of Hamilton, IL. is open for tours year round. The *Hancock County Courthouse* in Carthage is on the National Register of Historic Places.

Burlington to Keokuk, IA, and Fort Madison to Nauvoo, IL

NAUVOO WILDLIFE OBSERVATION AREA is a wood duck sanctuary along *STH 96* just down river from Nauvoo. The ducks nest in large wooden boxes found along the highway and 15 to 20 feet high in trees in the state park.

BREEZEWOOD CAMPGROUND (4 miles south of Nauvoo on *STH 96*). 23 acres, adjacent to the Mississippi River. Swimming pool · nature trails · game room · store · laundromat · playground · electricity

---

SPECIAL EVENTS

"City of Joseph" Nauvoo, 1st week in August. Dramatic outdoor musical production based on the life of Joseph Smith. Accommodations must be reserved in advance as 35,000 to 45,000 people will attend. Considered to be one of the top 3 outdoor productions in America.

Grape Festival, Nauvoo State Park, Labor Day weekend. Parade Saturday and Sunday. Carnival, arts/crafts, flea market. Includes French rite, "Wedding of the cheese and wine."

Threshing Bee and Antique Show, Hamilton, IL. First weekend in August. Displays of working antique farm machinery.

The twelve mile drive along STH 96 between Nauvoo and Hamilton is considered to be one of the more scenic stretches of Illinois' Great River Road. Almost parklike, with several scenic waysides. The river flows directly beside the highway.

MONTEBELLO CONSERVATION AREA. 33 acres south of Lock & Dam 19 just above Hamilton, IL. Picnicking · fishing · boat launch

WILDCAT SPRINGS (Hamilton, IL). Camping·fishing·nature trails · ballfields · playground · swimming pool · picnicking

Hamilton, Illinois
Population 3,500

Located at the Illinois end of the fabled Keokuk Dam, on *STH 96* and *USH 136.* Hamilton was settled in 1833. Excellent view of Lock & Dam 19 and the Union Electric Power Plant. In the winter, bald eagles congregate over the open water to collect fish injured when going through the locks.

CHANEY CREEK ACCESS   Boat Launch, Hamilton, IL.

Warsaw, Illinois

Warsaw overlooks the Mississippi from bluffs where two government forts were located during the War of 1812 with Great Britain. Most of the village is listed in the National Register of Historic Places. Many of the buildings date from the late 19th century.

Like many other towns in the area, Warsaw creeks have long been the source of beautiful crystal geodes. Thus Warsaw was once known as the "Crystal City on the Point."

FORT EDWARDS STATE HISTORICAL SITE at Warsaw. A 50 foot granite shaft commemorates the Centennial of Fort Edwards. Overlooks the Mississippi River at "the Point."

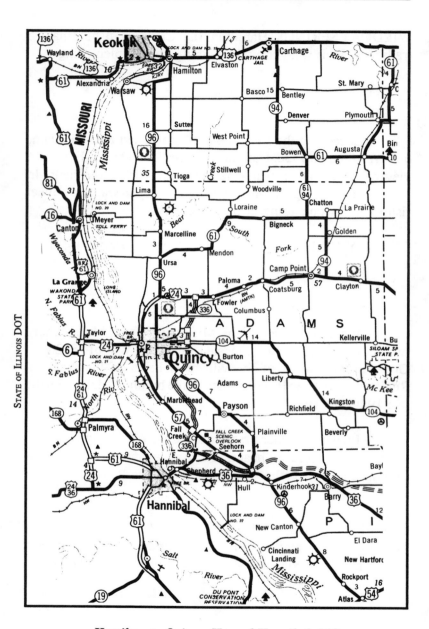

Hamilton to Quincy, IL, and Hannibal, MO

ADAMS COUNTY

Quincy, Illinois

MEYER'S LANDING FEDERAL RECREATION AREA (Near Lock & Dam 20, between Lima and Marcellina, IL). Car ferry to Canton, MO, operates from this landing.

BEAR CREEK FEDERAL RECREATION AREA (Turn west off *STH 96* at Marcelline, IL. Proceed 2 miles, turn left and drive 1/2 mile. Then turn right and follow the road 4 miles. Area is located 1/2 mile beyond the levee.) Camping·dump station·picnicking·boat launch into Pool 21

CANTON CHUTE FEDERAL RECREATION AREA (Proceed north from Quincy, IL, on Bay View Road approximately 4 miles. Turn left (west) on blacktop road and proceed for 3 miles.) No camping, boat launch only.

Quincy, Illinois
Population 39,681

For the traveler, Quincy might best be considered as a "hub" city. Though its stately, tree-lined streets, many parks, and abundant architectural treasures make it a pleasant destination, it is also centrally located to Nauvoo, Hannibal, and the recreational resources of the Mississippi River. Numerous hotels are found downtown, between 3rd and 5th streets.

VILLA KATHERINE VISITOR CENTER (532 Gardner Expressway). This Moorish castle on the banks of the Mississippi is certainly unique to the river. It was built in 1900 by international traveler and Quincy native, George Metz. Though modeled after the Villa Ben Abben in northern Algeria, the home incorporates various architectural features of the Alhambra, the Mosque of Thais, and the Alcazar. Request the handout for a self-guided tour. Tourism information is available.

While the new Bayview Bridge carries *USH 24* westward into Missouri, there are no major freeways through Quincy. Regardless, it has flourished through the years as an industrial center in the middle of an agricultural area. At one point it was nicknamed "Forgotonia" for the legendary self-sufficient attitude of its manufacturing and industrial magnates.

Flour and saw mills took early advantage of the rich grain production of neighboring fields, and the great forests of oak, walnut, and hickory gracing its bluffs. Such resources also led to Quincy being referred to as *Gem City.* In 1825, Quincy was the most northerly post office on the Mississippi River.

Villa Katherine Visitor Center

A Brief History of Quincy

The town of Quincy was originally called Bluffs as it was the only town site for 150 miles where the bluffs came directly to the waterline. Quincy was renamed to commemorate the 1825 inauguration of *John Quincy Adams* as the 6th President of the United States. The county was named Adams and, to complete the trilogy, the city park was named John's Square (now Washington Park).

Founder John Wood arrived from New York in 1821 to investigate a friend's land grant in this *Illinois Military Tract* which reached from the Mississippi to the Illinois River. Wood chose this site in part because the harbor would be sufficiently deep even in low water.

Quincy's harbor is the largest natural harbor on the Upper Mississippi River. Like the harbor built at Dubuque, it sheltered steamboats from moving ice during the winter. Records indicate that as many as 2,200 steamboats spent the winter in the Quincy Harbor.

Early on there was so little population north of Quincy that most steamboats carried only freight. By the 1840s, however, steamers were full of passengers, each line vying to outdo the other in size, luxurious accommodation, outstanding presentation and bounty in meals, and speed.

According to a Quincy businessman, B.H. Miller, interviewed in 1915, *"A trip to Keokuk, Burlington, Rock Island or one of the northern cities was a charming one. The scenery along the great father of waters is not excelled in beauty by any on earth. Passengers would crowd the decks with their telescopes and notebooks. Other would be seen sketching the beautiful hills and landscapes as they passed along. The ride from Keokuk to St. Louis began at 7 a.m. and was a 24 hour from journey. The fastest time on record between St. Louis and St. Paul was 800 miles in two days and 20 hours. ''* The Civil War sounded the death knell of the north/south oriented steamboatson the Mississippi River.

What to see in Qunicy

JOHN WOOD MANSION (425 S. 12th Street) Now a Historical Society Museum, this beautiful Gothic Revival wood frame mansion was built in 1835 for John Wood, the founder of Quincy. The home was moved piece by piece from across the street over a makeshift bridge which protected the 8-foot high *Osage Orange* hedge which encircled the yard. The home is on the National Register of Historic Places. Quincy offers nine other historical museums and several Historic Districts. Gift shop · small admission fee for museum.

Wood brought in German craftsmen to work on the mansion, offering them land and a home in exchange for their efforts. As more Germans came northward on steamboats from New Orleans, manufacturing flourished and two new breweries were established. The German neighborhood is now the *Calftown*

Historic District at State and 8th streets. A 5-story brick brewhouse is located at 9th and York streets. The city has entered into a sister-city relationship with Herford, Germany.

Wood's mansion is located in the East End Historic District along State

Greek Revival Wood Mansion

Street. Look for Italianate, Gothic, Richardsonian, 2nd Empire, and Queen Anne styles here and throughout the city.

HISTORIC DISTRICTS are abundant in this city. Like Galena to the north, this wealthy commercial center had a turn-of-the-century population which was nearly double that of today. Many of the homes are still owned by descendants of the original owners. Beautiful mansions, many dating from 1850 to 1910, brick streets, and limestone curbing still grace city neighborhoods.

National Geographic Magazine once described the corner of 16th and Maine as *the most architecturally significant corner in the U.S.* Quincy claims to have more different styles of architecture than anywhere outside of Chicago.

QUINCY MUSEUM OF NATURAL HISTORY AND ART (located in the Newcomb-Stillwell mansion completed in 1891. 1601 Maine Street). This major city museum includes exhibits of American Indian artifacts, fossils, minerals, animal specimens, and a children's discovery room. The first floor has been restored to the style of the 1890s. The massive stone building includes exquisite stone carving throughout the exterior. It is interesting to note that this mansion was built by a paper industry industrialist who started from scratch in Quincy after losing everything he owned in the Chicago Fire. Small admission fee.

GARDNER MUSEUM OF ARCHITECTURE AND DESIGN (4th and Maine streets). Formerly the Quincy Public Library, completed in 1888. The museum features a permanent collection of stained glass windows from Quincy's churches, as well as various temporary exhibits that include architecturally significant aspects of Quincy's past. Open 1-5 p.m. weekends. Small admission fee.

Newcomb-Stillwell Mansion, Quincy Museum of Natural History and Art

ALL WARS MUSEUM (at 1701 North 12th Street on the grounds of the Illinois Veterans Home). Displays of military memorabilia. Open 9-11 a.m. and 1-4 p.m. weekends. 1-4 p.m. Wednesday through Friday. Open holidays. Free.

WASHINGTON PARK (Between 4th and 5th on Maine). Farmers' market May through October on Tuesday and Saturday. A lovely city square that was called John's Square until 1857.

A bronze statue in Washington Park marks the site of the sixth of seven *Lincoln-Douglas Debates* in 1858. It is estimated that 15,000 people gathered here during the U.S. Senate campaign to hear Abraham Lincoln argue that slavery must be contained in existing slave-states. Stephen A. Douglas, a Quincy resident, expressed for the first time his belief that *"civilized men should be allowed to decide for themselves whether or not they wanted slavery."*

Douglas was reelected to the Senate after the debate. Two years later, Lincoln was nominated as the Republican presidential candidate.

THE UNDERGROUND RAILROAD

Quincyans were, for the most part, abolitionists. The town, because of its proximity to the shores of Missouri, was known to be one of four major routes for the *underground railroad* whereby slaves were ferreted out of Missouri and on to freedom in Canada.

Slave trade had always been an accepted part of life in Missouri, as many settlers had arrived from Kentucky and Tennessee with their families and all their earthly possessions --including their slaves. Though congregations and families often were divided, abolitionist preachers and sympathetic businessmen were asked to leave Missouri.

Missouri, bordered by three free states (Illinois, Iowa, and Kansas) was considered to be a ''peninsula of slavery jutting into a sea of freedom.'' Insurance companies insured against losses from runaway slaves and penalties were severe for those aiding in the escape of slaves. Vigilante Committees routinely patrolled the Mississippi River shorelines, freeing any unlocked or unlicensed boat and checking wagons for stowaways.

The main freedom route led west of Missouri to Lawrence, KS, and then north into central Iowa where the Quakers played a major role in establishing and maintaining the railroad. Alton, IL, under the direction of Elijah Lovejoy, and Quincy, IL, were two other major routes.

From Quincy, the route led through Galesburg, IL, then on to Chicago. One Quincy sympathizer was credited with facilitating the departure of 300 slaves, and there were 42 other known operators in Adams County. Two young college students from Quincy, caught aiding two slaves, were sentenced to twelve years in prison. The owner reported that the slaves *"would not be taking any more frolics of this nature in the near future."*

For the most part, very little documentation exists regarding the railroad. Laws strictly prohibited and severely punished those aiding slaves. Strict confidence was required which meant that even children often were not aware of their parents' activities. Hollow walls, hollow haystacks, and wood-piles often served as way stations. Those who were active felt they were opposing a morally corrupt system.

When the Civil War did break out, Quincy, situated as it was on the extreme western edge of Illinois and projecting into the state of Missouri, held a position of importance in Illinois that was second only to Cairo. Companies gathered here to be organized and about 800 soldiers could be cared for in Quincy hospitals. Many black men enlisted here to join Col. Gross and a Massachusetts regiment, or the 29th Colored Regiment.

THE QUINCY BAYVIEW BRIDGE over the Mississippi River has a unique computer-designed cable construction to allow an extra-wide center span. Barges require this extra-wide span to negotiate a sharp river bend to the west at this spot.

QUINSIPPI ISLAND, 130 acres, contains a reconstructed pioneer village, furnished and restored to depict life of early settlers (open during special festivals). An antique auto museum at Front and Cedar streets is open on Sundays from Memorial Day to Labor Day.

The Quincy Bayview Bridge

While down on Front Street, a fun place to stop for a bit of fresh batter-fried river carp and catfish is the Sky Ride Inn. The sign above the door of the adjacent River House Bar proclaims in large letters the number 327.3. This is a river mile marker indicating the river mile at which Quincy is located. The river mile markers for the Upper Mississippi commence at Cairo, IL. River miles for all major towns and landmarks along the river are listed in the Appendix, page 234.

BOB BANGERT PARK is a riverfront park at the northwest edge of town which offers picnicking, playground, and boat launch. Additional boat launches available at Quincy Bay and the Squaw Chute Marina.

WAVERING AQUATIC CENTER (north 36th Street). Pool · picnicking · tennis courts

RIVERVIEW PARK (on the Bluff at north edge of town). Statue of George Rogers Clark · picnicking · playground · benches for river watching

George Rogers Clark

The statue at Riverview Park commemorates a little known player in the fortunes of Mississippi River settlers and the infant American nation. While rebellious eastern colonists grappled with the English army in the east, settlers in the western frontiers (Kentucky and Tennesse) faced constant harassment from the British-allied native Indians.

George Rogers Clark entered the Revolutionary War scene as the head of Kentucky's irregular militia where he specialized in defending against Indian attacks. He traced the source of Indian uprisings to British Emissaries at Kaskaskia, Vincennes, Detroit, and other spots. He was one of the first Americans to fully comprehend the advantages of an American conquest to the banks of the Mississippi River.

In July of 1778, Clark helped convince Thomas Jefferson of the Commonwealth of Virginia to provide him with men and supplies with which to fight British influence on the Mississippi River. Clark left Louisville with 153 men and orders to attack the French village at Kaskaskia, (IL). The careful coaching by the British as to the inhuman nature of the Americans backfired when, paralyzed by the "hideous cries" of Clark's small company, the French residents refused to offer any resistance.

After being treated by Clark with the most gentle diplomacy, these good citizens in turn calmed their frightened kins-folk at Cahokia, who happily switched allegiance to America. In like bloodless manner, the French at Vincennes surrendered to the legendary "Long Knives" of Kentucky and Tennessee, thereby giving the U.S. claim to all lands north of the Ohio River, east of the Mississippi River, and south of the Great Lakes. As a result of this bloodless coup, the great region officially became a part of the Commonwealth of Virginia.

Clark later was asked to explore the Louisiana Purchase, but Clark, by then in his 50s, suggested that his younger brother, William, lead the expedition to the Pacific Ocean.

Follow STH 57 south to STH 336 and follow Hannibal exits onto USH 36 to Hannibal, MO

LOCK & DAM 21 offers a new observation platform and ranger-led tours of the dam. Boat launch nearby.

JOHN HAY FEDERAL RECREATION AREA (Located on the Illinois side of *USH 36* under the bridge to Hannibal, MO). Camping (no electric) · boat launch · picnicking

PARK-N-FISH FEDERAL RECREATION AREA (Proceed 7 miles west of Hull, IL on *USH 36,* turn south on gravel road for 6.2 miles to the area. Near Lock & Dam 22). 6 camp sites · water · picnicking

LOCK AND DAM 22 (Travel south from Hannibal, MO, 7 miles on *STH 79* to the Saverton exit and follow signs). No camping. Boat launch only.

FALL CREEK SCENIC OVERLOOK AND REST AREA (Off *STH 57,* 12 miles south of Quincy). Picnicking · overlook · trails · native prairie plants

ICE HARVESTING ON THE MISSISSIPPI RIVER

The river industry which lasted longer than any other except for commercial fishing was ice harvesting. Ice was cut from the river, stored in layers separated by sawdust, and sold during the warmer months. The job was largely seasonal, with a large plant near Hannibal, MO, employing perhaps 150 men during the winter cutting season. As a rule each of the small towns north of Hannibal had several ice houses. The larger companies shipped ice to St. Louis and other southern cities. Stored ice was also sold to steamboat crews and railroads for refrigeration of their perishable cargo or for passenger needs

Ice thickness in this area generally ranged from 8 to 14 inches. Any snow which had collected on top of the ice from the beginning of the freezing weather had to be removed. If the

Ice Harvesting on the Mississippi River

snow was several inches deep, it was cleaned with a scraper pulled by horses and piled on shore. Extremely light snow was swept by men with brooms.

After snow removal, the ice was carefully scored in long lines the length of the ice field to be harvested. In the early days, a horse pulled a device which had several prongs spaced 24 inches apart which would gouge a groove almost an inch deep. This made a visible mark for the men sawing the ice into uniform slabs, 24" wide by 40" long. At later dates, scoring was done with a gasoline powered machine.

As soon as the field was properly cleaned and scored, the cutting began. Until some time after 1900, ice was cut by hand with a one-man saw about five feet long with teeth an inch or more in length. The ice cut fairly easily, but a full day of pushing the saw and dragging it back was a grueling task.

The first ice cut started at the icehouse ramp which carried the ice from the river up an incline into the ice house. The first cut was 36 inches wide and started a single open water canal or sluice which extended to the outer edge of the ice field. The regular cakes of ice were only 24 inches across and could be easily pushed or pulled through the canal.

Many men would be sawing ice at the same time. A continuous series of blocks floated through the canal toward the ice house for storage. The blocks were helped along by a group of men somewhat evenly spaced along the canal, using long poles with gaff hooks to pull or push the blocks along their route.

The Creve Coeur Lake Ice Company operated in Scipio, MO, north of Hannibal, until 1906. The company could harvest 3,100 tons of ice per week and warehouse 17,000 tons.

By 1906, artificial ice was coming into use, and experiments in mechanical refrigeration were discussed and foreseen. A last cement warehouse built in Scipio in 1909 proved unsuitable for ice storeage--the ice fused together into one big lump. It reportedly it took a full year for the ice chunk to melt away. That closed the chapter on the thirty-eight year old ice industry in Scipio.

Author's Note: Much of the history on Quincy's underground railroad, the Hannibal history in the next chapter, and the special feature on *Ice Harvesting,* comes from Hurley and Roberta Hagood, historians and authors from Hannibal, MO. This young couple, who freely admit to "pushing 80," have made a major contribution to recording the history of the Hannibal area. As authors of *Hannibal, Too,* and other books, they have donated copyrights to various organizations so that they are not personally profiting from their publications.

"People trust us," Roberta says, *"were we to profit, I don't think people would be nearly as forthcoming with pictures, maps and other original documents. We're retired from careers that paid us well. Our concern is mainly to get this information recorded for future generations."*

The University of Iowa has already microfiched nearly *20,000* 6x4 inch notecards of historical data and sources recorded by Roberta in the course of her research.

The boyhood home of
Mark Twain

Hannibal, Missouri
See map, p. 201

THE NEW MADRID EARTHQUAKE OF 1811

While much of the nation expects the next "big one" to occur in California, many scientists feel there is an equal chance that an earthquake of major proportions will occur along the *New Madrid Fault* (locally pronounced New MAD-rid) in the Mississippi and Ohio river valleys.

It is here that the most devastating earthquake to occur in the United States took place in 1811-1812 at New Madrid in southeastern Missouri. The quake occurred before any significant settlement of the area, but the tremors were felt as far away as Detroit and Washington D.C. Trees fell, bluffs and cabins tumbled. Large areas of bedrock were uplifted while entire islands sank. *Reelfoot Lake* (just south and east of New Madrid, in Tennessee) formed when 20,000 acres sank ten feet and caused the Mississippi River to flow backwards.

The few settlers who lived along the river found their riverside farms swallowed up or buried in sand which spewed from the earth. They benefited from one of the first attempts of the young nation to provide social welfare. In 1815, Congress passed an act to relieve landowners who lost property by allowing resettlement on a similar tract of public land.

More than 500 earthquake certificates redeemable for up to 640 acres of any government land were distributed. *In 1819, Abraham Bird exchanged his earthquake certificate for land at the present site of Hannibal, Mo.*

Hannibal, Missouri
Population 18,000

As the boyhood home of Samuel Langhorne Clemens-- better known as Mark Twain, author of *Tom Sawyer, Huckleberry Finn* and other well known books--Hannibal is one of the few river towns that is truly a national tourism destination. Attendance at the annual *Tom Sawyer Days* festival puts Hannibal among the 10 most popular 4th of July destinations in the United States. The neon lights, the trinkets, the festive air about town announce it as an American Mecca.

There can be no doubt as to the source of this national significance. Enter from the Illinois side and the traveler is rising over the river on the iron Mark Twain Memorial Bridge built in 1936. Then there is the Mark Twain Hotel built in 1905, the new Clemens Best Western, the Becky Thatcher Bookstore, the Mark Twain Book Store, Huck Finn *this,* Tom Sawyer *that... .*

The town setting is still picturesque, with homes built right up the bluffs from the river. Follow *USH 36 west* to *USH 61 south* and around town to find the hotels and restaurants and the *Missouri State Visitors Center.* Streets in the town are numbered away from the river, with 2nd Street being Main Street.

Twain's childhood home *(1)* from 1844 to 1853 is located at 208 Hill Street. The white clapboard house was fully restored during 1990. The nearby corner of Hill and Main is the historic commercial area of old Hannibal. When Sam Clemens was young, 'pig drives' still occurred on Hill Street. No doubt young Clemens participated in the roundups of runaway pigs which netted the boys 25 cents for each animal.

Adjoining Twain's home is the *Mark Twain Museum* which is filled with Twain and Tom Sawyer memorabilia. Note especially 16 *Norman Rockwell paintings* produced to illustrate *Tom Sawyer* and *Huckleberry Finn.* Displays and slide show in the nearby visitor center *(2)* focus on Mark Twain's days in Hannibal. Public restrooms available. All Mark Twain Museum facilities are open daily, summers from 8 a.m. to 6 p.m.; November through March, 9 a.m. to 4 p.m.

For the visitor, boning up on your Tom Sawyer and Huckleberry Finn is essential, for half the fun of visiting Hannibal lies in making the leap between fact and fiction.

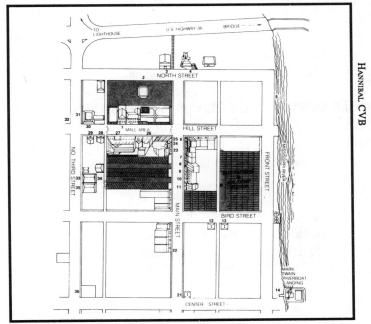

A Walking Tour of Mark Twain's Hannibal

Things to See in Hannibal (Keyed to Walking Tour Map)

NIPPER PARK, *(15)* at the river end of Broadway. Marina · playground · river views

MARK TWAIN HOTEL built in 1905 as the town's first tribute to Twain. Supposedly the location of Tom Sawyer's old swimming hole.

FLOOD MARK on the Hannibal National Bank (Main & Broadway). The Hannibal National Bank on Main St. has provided rowing service through many floods, the worst of which was the 1973 flood, which is commemorated with a black line about four feet high at the front entrance to the bank.

The flooding which has plagued the commercial district of town will be brought under control as the new 13 foot high flood wall is completed on the riverfront. Three large gates provide access through the wall to the riverfront. It is interesting to note that as river towns build high flood walls, towns across the river tend to build higher levees and walls as well!

VISIT UPSTAIRS DISPLAYS AT BUSINESSES (*27 & 28* bookstores, drugstore) neighboring Mark Twain's boyhood home. The shops each have a diorama from one of Twain's famous books about his boyhood in Hannibal. No charge.

MARK TWAIN Riverboat Cruises (*14*, Center Street Landing). Summer sightseeing cruises daily at 11 a.m., 1:30 and 4 p.m. No reservation necessary. Board for dinner cruises at 6:30. Fall and spring schedules vary. Reservation suggested for dinner. Call 314-221-3222 or 800-621-2322.

The *Delta Queen* and *Mississippi Queen* excursion steamboats stop at Hannibal's levee *(5)* on a regularly announced morning schedule throughout the summer. Though visitors are usually not allowed on board the huge paddlewheelers, the boats are a sight to behold. Expect a rousing calliope concert to accompanying the swooshing of the great red paddlewheel at departure.

CARDIFF HILL *(4)*. The bronze statues of Huck and Tom are located at the base of Cardiff Hill. A statue of Mark Twain and a Light House dedicated to the author are atop the hill.

RIVERVIEW PARK (*USH 36 west* onto Harrison Hill). Several scenic overlooks with a large playground and picnicking area located near the exit (behind the waterworks building). Visitors may notice that the one-way traffic is led to the left rather than the right. The designer of the park was English.

MISSOURI STATE VISITOR CENTER and numerous motels and restaurants are located on *USH 61*. It is wise to make reservations for lodging before arriving in Hannibal, particularly after June 1 and certainly when attending annual festivals or holidays.

ROCKCLIFFE MANSION (1000 Bird Street). The home of lumber magnate, John Cruikshank from 1900 until 1924. This National Historic Site has been carefully restored and furnished. Its experimental art deco style was a break from the Victorian traditions of its time. Guided tours daily except Thanksgiving, Christmas, New Year's Day. Small Fee

MARK TWAIN CAVE (located 1 mile south of Hannibal on *STH 79*). Discovered in 1819, and doubtless explored by young Sam Clemens, this cave has been designated as a *U.S. National Landmark*. Guided tours, 55 minutes long, leave the visitor center every 15 minutes.

CAMERON CAVE (1-1/4 hour long guided tours leave the Mark Twain Cave visitor center at 10 a.m., noon, 1:30 and 3 p.m.). Several visitors on the tour carry lanterns during this tour of a complex maze cave. Open Memorial Day to Labor Day.

LOVERS LEAP is the 250 foot high rock bluff just south of Hannibal. Well worth visiting on the way to Mark Twain's Cave. Good road to the scenic overlook.

Rock faces exposed in the Hannibal area vary from 20 to 50 million years old. Lovers Leap, located just south of Hannibal's riverfront, offers the most visible sampling of area limestone. From the bottom to the top, gray to dark gray *Saverton Shale* resembles smooth mud, followed by blocky looking *Louisiana Limestone,* light gray *Hannibal Shale* that breaks off in plates. At the top, dark brown *Burlington Limestone* with veins of white "chert" used as flint by the Indians.

The red sand hills at the south edge of Hannibal were deposited by the *Kansan and Nebraskan glaciers* slightly less that 1 million years ago.

A Brief History of Hannibal

Hannibal does have a rather significant history outside of Tom Sawyer and Huckleberry Finn! The first settler in the area is considered to be Moses D. Bates, a carpenter who came up river from St. Louis. He and two other men cleared a site located at the foot of what is now Hill Street. They named their settlement, Hannibal, the name originally given to *Bear Creek* by a Spanish surveyor in 1800 .

Hannibal was the great African general who, for 30 years, beginning in 225 B.C., led the forces of Carthage against

---

SPECIAL EVENTS

Winter Bluegrass Festival, Mid-February, Hannibal. Nationally known bluegrass music and entertainment.

Annual Farm Toy Show, 4th weekend in February, Hannibal. Exhibits feature antique and new farm toys. Auction held on Saturday.

Mississippi River Art Fair, Memorial Day Weekend, Nipper Park.

National Tom Sawyer Days, early July, Hannibal. Celebration focuses on such family fun as the National Fence Painting Championships, frog jumping competitions, Arts and Crafts Show, stage entertainment, dancing, food, and July 4th fireworks display at the riverfront.

Autumn Historic Folklife Festival, 3rd weekend in October, Hannibal. Artisans demonstrate crafts of the mid-1800s. Musicians, storytellers, food prepared over open fires.

Spain. His crossing of the Alps on 37 war elephants was only one of several highly creative battle plans. *Scipio* was the Roman war general who attacked and eventually defeated the Carthaginians. It was a later surveyor who gave the name of Scipio to the settlement one mile north of Hannibal.

Through the years, Hannibal's economic prosperity has revolved around a series of major industries: lumber, railroads, shoes, and cement.

The lumbering era flourished from the 1840s to 1906. Hannibal, at one time, claimed to be the 4th largest lumbering center in the U.S. Great rafts of logs from the north were floated into the Bear Creek valley, sawed into lumber, and shipped in all directions on the river or by rail. Lumber yards occupied nearly every square foot of land from Bay Island to Bear Creek and right through the valley. Lumber piles from 20 to 25 feet high lined the river front. The North Missouri Lumber Company, in operation today, began as a sawmill in 1819.

By the late 1800s, Hannibal was the largest rail center west of the Mississippi. In 1846, Judge John Marshall Clemens, the father of Samuel Langhorne Clemens, was instrumental in establishing the *Hannibal & St. Joseph Railroad*. As the first railroad to cross Missouri to St. Joseph at the edge of the western frontier, it provided transportation and supplies to western settlers. St. Joseph was also the starting point for the *Pony Express* whose riders carried the mail to California. A new idea for sorting the mail enroute from Hannibal reduced transit time of overland mail by 14 hours.

John Garth was a founder of the *Universal Atlas/ Portland Cement Company* which opened a plant in Hannibal in 1901. With workers brought in from Poland, Romania, Hungary and other Slavic countries, the company provided all the cement for the Keokuk Dam in 1913, the Panama Canal in 1903, the Empire State building, and many of the buildings in Chicago after the fire in 1871.

B&B fans will enjoy the *Garth Woodside Mansion*. The mansion served as a summer home to John Garth and his family. The proprietors

Garth Woodside Mansion

have added their personal antique collection to the Garth's original furnishings. The congenial atmosphere, wooded grounds with a stocked fishing pond, museum quality furnishings, and gourmet breakfast make this one of the nation's finest B&Bs. Reservations suggested!

Agriculture, of course, has always been a major industry in the area. Flour milling was significant until after World War 1, when fewer biscuits and hot breads were baked at home. As early as 1847, 14,000 hogs were slaughtered in Hannibal. Cattle, hemp, and tobacco all were important in the agricultural economy.

Campgrounds Near Hannibal

Bayview Campers Park. (1 mile from city limits, north on *Route 168,* 3 miles.) Open year around. Swimming pool · rec hall · shower · laundromat · miniature golf · playground · grocery · canoe rental · electric hookups · dump station

Injun Joe Campground & Water Slide. (At Clemens Landing, south of Hannibal on *USH 61,* 4 miles). Pool · waterslide · go-carts · restaurant · live outdoor theatre · electric & sewer · laundromat · grocery · wooded tent area

Mark Twain Cave Campground. (Located at Mark Twain Cave Park, 1 mile south of Hannibal on *STH 79.)* Lots of grass and shade · full hookups · tent area · laundry · dump station · groceries

Mark Twain Lake State Park (*USH 36 west onto Route J,* 30 miles from Hannibal). Numerous state and private campgrounds and resorts in Missouri's largest state park.

Valley View Campground (2300 N. Bayview Dr. North edge of Quincy, IL, off *USH 24)* Boat launch · full hookups

INSIGHT

HENRY SWEETS
Curator, Mark Twain Museum

"*I think it's interesting to note that Mark Twain lived in Hartford, Connecticut, far longer than the 13 years he was in Hannibal. Yet far more people (130,000 a year) visit the Mark Twain Museum in this little rivertown. I really believe that is because people are coming to visit Tom Sawyer, not Mark Twain.*

"*As a boy, Twain revelled in the excitement of a steamboat arrival, the coming of the railroad, the lumber years. He really did prowl through damp limestone caverns and scramble up the side of Cardiff hill. Tom Sawyer and Huckleberry Finn are such great stories because Mark Twain grew up at such a picturesque time in Mississippi River history. His characters were modeled after real people who later took pride in claiming their particular character. The caves, islands, bluff tops and riverboats that Twain wrote of can still be explored by the visitor.*

"*The stories themselves are timeless. Even though fences are almost never whitewashed any more, we can all relate to how clever it was of Tom to trick his friends into doing the chore. It's something we all wish we had done ourselves.*

"*I see myself as a 'street historian' rather than a Mark Twain scholar. My observations regard more how people relate to Twain than how a scholar does. For example, there are two sets of Norman Rockwell paintings at the Museum. One set depicts scenes from* **Huckleberry Finn,** *the other from* **Tom Sawyer.**

"*What I notice is, that as visitors linger over the scenes from Tom Sawyer, they identify the incidents and characters from the story, 'There's Aunt Polly.' 'There's the cave where they got lost.' 'There's Sid.'*

"*When they get to the scenes from Huckleberry Finn, they say, 'Oh, there's Norman Rockwell!' So while scholars might say* **Huckleberry Finn** *was Twain's greatest work, it would appear to me that people have enjoyed and remembered more from* **Tom Sawyer** *than from Huck Finn. For this reason, I have no problem with calling Clemens' mother's room Aunt Polly's room. The two are interchangeable for the public. Mark Twain is Tom Sawyer.*

"*It's challenging, too, because whenever anyone has a difficult Twain question, we are expected to know everything there is to know about Twain or any character in any of his books. The most fun is when we get a call to verify some obscure Twain comment, for example when the* Reader's Digest *editors called to verify where it was that Twain wrote the line, 'It's deliciousness itself.' That's a toughy, but we found it in* **Life on the Mississippi.**

"*We've had our surprises, too. For example, in researching for the current restoration of Twain's boyhood home, we made the discovery that Twain's house had actually shrunk since the days Twain lived here. The 1st floor kitchen and upstairs back bedroom had been removed. Twain had actually made that comment publicly in 1902--that the house seemed to have shrunk--but until now, nobody realized that it had been remodeled on a smaller scale with the same general layout. It really had shrunk!*"

The "Unsinkable" Molly Brown

Hannibal has no shortage of memorable characters in its recent past. The "Unsinkable" Molly Brown was born Margaret Tobin Brown in 1867 in a small home on Denkler's Alley. According to local lore, her adventures began well before her experience on the Titanic and followed her well after.

As a young child, she was swept from the riverfront onto the island opposite Hannibal by a tornado. Mark Twain, a distant relative visiting the island, is reported to have found her, shaken and muddy. Twain helped the youngster up and muttered, "Where am I going to find you next!" Many years later, as a young woman, she is reputed to have asked Twain how she, too, might become *Rich and Famous*. His reply was that it couldn't happen in Hannibal and that her best bet was to go west and marry a gold miner.

In fact, Molly and her brother did go west, and she did marry a mining superintendent. A gold strike made her rich beyond her wildest dreams. According to the story, her first husband died a violent death as did a second, leaving Molly certainly *rich,* but craving *fame.* A country girl, and considered loud and uncouth, Molly was disdained by the wealthy Denver Society she sought to cultivate.

While vacationing in Europe in 1912, she heard that John Jacob Astor and much of the nation's "high society" would be aboard the maiden voyage of the Titanic. Seeing an opportunity to wine and dine a captive audience, Molly, too, bought tickets for the ill-fated voyage.

When an iceberg ripped a hole in the Titanic, Molly distinguished herself by unselfishly helping women and children board lifeboats until she was forced off the sinking ship. Once in a boat, she encouraged her companions by rowing, singing, etc. Rescued four hours later, she continued selflessly to help the other survivors. It was her selfless effort on the behalf of others that made Molly Brown one of the most *famous* of the Titanic survivors.

Molly Brown went on to survive two more shipwrecks, a typhoon, and a disastrous fire at a Palm Beach Hotel. As she cooly descended the hotel stairs she commented to reporters, "After all I've been through, you can't blame me if this all seems a little routine!" Also known as the Salamander Lady, Molly died a bitter recluse. For all her fame and fortune, she was never accepted by high society.

"A true story?" I asked the shopkeeper who had related Molly's story so enthusiastically.

"The line between fact and fiction often seems to blur in Hannibal," he grinned, *"but, yes, we believe it to be true."*

Another Hannibal native, "Old Eagle Eye" Jake Beckly is buried in Riverside Cemetery. Jake was born in 1867 and played in baseball's major leagues until 1907. He totaled a major league average of .309 and collected 2,930 hits. He was inducted into the Baseball Hall of Fame in 1971.

Nearby Sites to Visit

MARK TWAIN LAKE and STATE PARK is located south-west of Hannibal and New London, MO. A man-made, 18,600 acre lake provides the setting for one of the major State Parks in eastern Missouri. Self-guided tours of Cannon Dam's main floor. See generators and displays. Several camping areas with a total of 450 sites. 80 sites at the Indian Creek Camp may be reserved. A full-scale resort is planned near Florida, MO, with lodging, marina, and golf.

MARK TWAIN BIRTHPLACE HISTORIC SITE (Florida, MO. South from Hannibal on *USH 61* to *STH 19* to *STH 154* to *STH 107*). The original Clemens log cabin is preserved, enclosed in a modern building overlooking Mark Twain Lake.

The Salt River
(adapted from the August 1988 *Hannibal Courier-Post*)

Several creeks, rivers, and tiny towns in this corner of Missouri have names relating to SALT, i.e.. Saverton and various "Licks." Spaulding Springs was originally known as Bouvet's Lick. Salt deposits left by ancient seas fueled some of the earliest forays and early settlements in the area.

Records first mention a French settlement at the site of a salt spring near present-day Saverton (south of Hannibal, on the Mississippi River) in 1774. Traders packed salt out in canoes to supply St. Louis with seasoning and salt for such industrial uses as packing/curing hides, meats, etc. It was a lucrative business but dangerous because of animosity between manufac-turers and native Indians. In 1799 another salt lick was estab-lished at Freemore's Lick just south of Saverton.

As the salt business became less lucrative the mineral rich springs were developed as health spas (as was Spaulding Springs) which were very popular after the turn of the century. Families often traveled great distances for long periods of time, perhaps years, in search of "healthful" waters.

The drive south from Hannibal, MO, along STH 79 to Alton, IL, contains the most striking bluff-country scenery south of Dubuque, IA. Below Lock & Dam 24, at Clarksville, MO, Pinnacle Peak soars to 600 feet high. The skyride at Pinnacle Peak and several roadside overlooks provide panoramic views of an ever-widening, island-ladened Mississippi River.

It has been speculated that bluffs found between Hannibal and Louisiana, MO, are foothills of the Ozark mountains found to the southwest. They generally are 250 feet high and composed mainly of various limestones and shales.

Early explorers would have found 14 to 20 different types of oak trees in the hills around Hannibal--and a thick layer of acorns 6 to 8" deep. Maple, ash, cottonwood, willows, haw, pecans and hickory are also abundant. According to local historian, Hurley Hagood, pigs were introduced in Iowa to eat the thick blanket of acorns (also called MAST) which layered the rolling hills and valleys. The covering of acorns and brush was so thick in the area that many winters the ground beneath did not freeze.

The flat, treeless prairie begins about ten miles west of Hannibal. Thick prairie grasses prevented tree seeds from reaching soil for germination.

Louisiana, MO, was named in 1817 to commemorate the Louisiana Purchase. Stark's Nursery, now the oldest nursery in the United States and the largest in the world, was established in 1818. Early immigrants to the area were almost all southern tobacco growers and by the early 1860s the city's economic wealth revolved around 14 cigar and related tobacco factories.

Pre-civil war homes abound. All the streets are named for states, so that a resident might live on Georgia, in Louisiana, Missouri.

Lover's Leap (aptly named!) overlooks the Mark Twain paddlewheeler on the Mississippi River. Exposed rock stratas are visible.

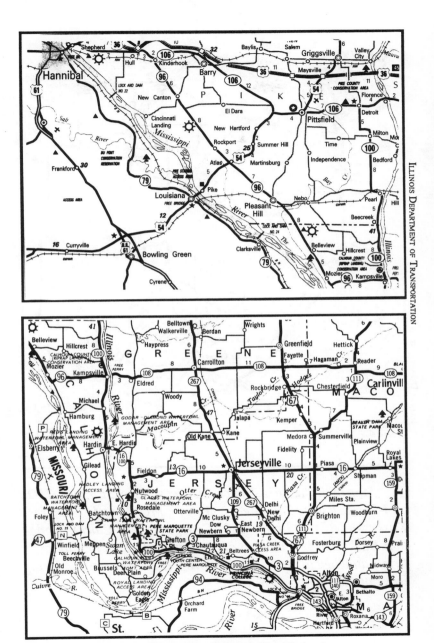

Hannibal, MO, to Kampsville, IL (top)
Kampsville to Alton, IL

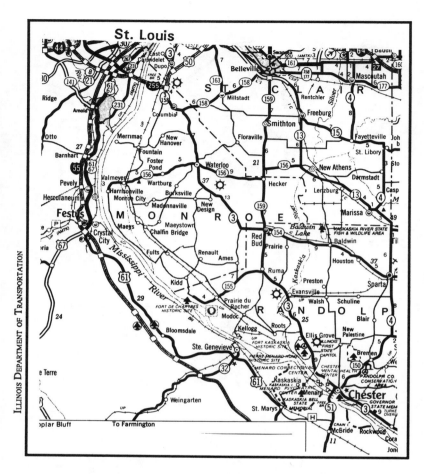

Map of the historic French District south of St. Louis, MO, on I-55. See page 209 (Ste. Genevieve, MO, Fort de Chartres, Kaskaskia, IL) and page 180 (George Rogers Clark). Notice that Kaskaskia is a portion of the state of Illinois that today is firmly attached to the Missouri shore, reflecting the meandering ways of the Father of Waters!

A Gathering Place of Waters
The American Bottoms

CALHOUN COUNTY, ILLINOIS

> The route suggested here follows *USH 54* east from Louisiana, MO, across the *Champ Clark Bridge* to Illinois *STH 96* and south through *Calhoun County* to Kampsville, IL, on the banks of the Illinois River. A free car ferry crosses the Illinois River at Kampsville, however, the Great River Road continues south on *STH 100* to cross the Illinois River at Hardin's unique lift bridge. *STH 100*, Illinois' Great River Road, continues south to Grafton, IL, through Jersey County.
>
> As a suggested alternate route, do not cross the Illinois River at Hardin, but drive straight south through Calhoun County on *STH 96* to the tiny town of Brussels (population 125).

Picturesque Calhoun County is located on a long penninsula of land between the Mississippi and Illinois rivers. Its fertile bottomland supports fields of corn and soybeans which are protected from flooding by levees. The rolling hills of Calhoun County bloom with extensive peach and apple orchards, blueberries, and raspberries. Several inviting tea rooms and restaurants are located in historic buildings on the peninsula. *(See map page 201.)*

McCULLY HERITAGE PROJECT near Kampsville, IL, offers woodland trails and revolving interpretive exhibits about the plant and animal life in the Illinois River valley.

THE CENTER FOR AMERICAN ARCHEOLOGY is located in Kampsville just one block off *STH 100.* A highway sign directs the traveler to the *Kampsville Museum,* open 10 a.m. to 5 p.m., Tuesday through Sunday, May through October. Excavation sites may be open during June and July. The museum contains educational exhibits about the Indian cultures which have occupied this area during the past 8,000 years. Also displayed are artifacts excavated at various sites in the lower Illinois River valley, the most famous being the *Koster Site* which closed in 1979.

Extensive trade networks among early Indian cultures mean almost anything can show up during an archeological dig. This figure found by "puddling" deep in the mud of the Mississippi River is believed to be a Mayan idol.

MARK TWAIN NATIONAL WILDLIFE REFUGE VISITOR CENTER, near the Brussels Car Ferry, provides visitor information and an excellent interpretive center staffed by Fish & Wildlife Service employees. There are nine waterfowl sanctuaries, with a total of 23,500 acres, under the protection of the National Fish and Wildlife Service in Illinois, Iowa, and Missouri. Observation deck with spotting scopes · scheduled tours into the bottomlands

THE ILLINOIS RIVER

Named for the Illini (Illiniwek) who, along with the Potowatomi and Kickapoo (Shawnee) Indians, occupied this area. August Chouteau, founder of St. Louis, purchased 10 million acres along the Illinois River from the Kickapoo Indians for the U.S. government in 1817.

The Illinois River begins 500 river miles northeast of here, near Chicago, IL. Barge traffic reaches north into central Illinois where at La Salle, IL, the *Illinois & Michigan Canal,* completed in 1848, once provided a 120-mile canal to Chicago. Today the Calumet-Sag channel north of Joliet completes a continuous waterway from the Mississippi to the Great Lakes and, via the St. Lawrence Seaway, to the Atlantic Ocean.

The renowned agricultural wealth of central Illinois has its source in the glacial drift which blankets the Illinois River valley to a depth of 20 to 200 feet. The valley is as broad as that of the Mississippi River, indicating that the Illinois River was once similar in size to the Mississippi River.

Grafton, IL, 20 miles south on *USH 100,* Illinois' *Great River Road.*

JERSEY COUNTY, ILLINOIS

Jersey County was established in 1839 and named to honor New Jersey, the home state of many of its immigrants. The area was called *the gathering place of waters* by Indians. It was the beginning of a vast, fertile floodplain now called the *American Bottoms.* This fertile crescent, looping about 90 miles to south of St. Louis, has been flooded again and again by highwaters of the Missouri, Illinois and Mississippi rivers.

STUMP LAKE WATER MANAGEMENT AREA located along *STH 100* just upriver from *Pere Marquette State Park.* Game preserve on the Illinois River. Hunting · fishing

PERE MARQUETTE STATE PARK (Located just north of Grafton along the Great River Road and the Illinois River). Illinois' largest state park (8,000 acres) offers good boating access to the Illinois River. Several scenic overlooks of the confluence of the Mississippi and Illinois rivers, their flood plains, and numerous islands. Dogwoods, redbuds, shadblow, wild cherry, and ornamental crabs are all in bloom in the park from April through May. Camping·swimming·equestrian trails

The limestone bluffs around Pere Marquette were up-lifted some 200 million years ago--even before the age of the dinosaurs. All the limestone ridges are mantled with windblown glacial loess. Watch for grassy hill prairies which crown many of the steepest hillsides.

The park lodge was constructed of native stone and timbers as a C.C.C. *(Civilian Conservation Corps)* project in the 1930s and was recently renovated at a cost of over 13 million dollars. A 12-foot square chess set in the main lounge has figures the size of children, and is believed to be the largest chess set in the world. A 700-ton stone fireplace presides over the dining area/lounge. Dining is excellent though visitors should plan to arrive EARLY for Sunday Brunch. Room reservations for summer weekends should be made well in advance.

High earthen mounds attributed to *Mississippian Indian cultures* are visible from the Great River Road. Archeological excavations in the area indicate prehistoric Indians occupied eighteen sites in the park. A village was located where the lodge now stands. Hunter/gatherers probably moved into the area as much as 2000 years ago with the *Cahokian cultural group* dominant in the 1300s.

> **5 miles to Grafton, IL**
> **25 miles to Alton, IL**

POHLMAN LAKE SLOUGH (located along the Mississippi River just south of the Illinois river). 94 acres of hunting and fishing.

THE FIN INN restaurant, just upriver of Grafton, boasts a huge 8,000-gallon native fish/turtle aquarium. White Perch is a specialty here, as is turtle soup--if you can eat it while watching resident specimens floating around the table-side aquarium. Note the bear-sized claws of the 150-pound alligator snapping turtle. Spoonbilled catfish is also available on the menu.

The French Colonial Period
1673 - 1763

A large granite cross just down river of Pere Marquette State Park on *STH 100* commemorates the landing of Father Jacques Marquette in 1673. Winter travelers will notice the large black nests of a Great Blue Heron rookery on a river island opposite this landmark. Sycamore, willow, and cottonwood trees are common in the river bottoms.

Pere Marquette and Louis Jolliet had followed the St. Lawrence Seaway, the Great Lakes, the Fox, Wisconsin and Mississippi rivers to arrive in this area. They continued as far south as Arkansas where they believed the Spanish to be active [they were not], then returned to this point where they followed the Illinois River back to the Great Lakes.

Marquette returned to Illinois in 1675 to establish the Jesuit Mission of the Immaculate Conception at the Kaskaskia Village near Starved Rock.

During 1680-81 Robert Cavelier Sieur de LaSalle traveled the entire length of the Illinois and Mississippi rivers. In 1682, LaSalle stood at the mouth of the Illinois River and claimed for France all of *"Louisiana (named for King Louis the 14th) from the mouth of the great river and the rivers that discharge themselves thereinto, from its source beyond the country of the Sioux Indians and as far as its mouth at the sea or the Gulf of Mexico."* La Salle and his lieutenant, Henri de Tonti, began the settlement of Illinois a few years later with the establishment of several forts along the Illinois River.

Around 1700, the French shifted their hold in Illinois to the Mississippi River. Several towns grew around Fort de Chartres, which had become the center of civic and military power by 1720.

In 1763 all French possessions east of the Mississippi River were ceded to Great Britain, causing many of the French colonists to move to Ste. Genevieve, now the oldest permanent settlement in Missouri. Unbeknownst to the residents, France had ceded the west bank to Spain.

Today, visitors can explore Ste. Genevieve (60 miles south of St. Louis on I-55), and Illinois' *Fort de Chartres State Historic Site*. The interpretive center on Main Street in Ste. Genevieve offers an excellent orientation with a slide show about historic Ste. Genevieve and a display about river history by the Army Corps of Engineers. Fifty buildings in Ste. Genevieve are more than 200 years old--seven of these are open to the public.

From Ste. Genevieve, a ferry crosses the Mississippi River to Modoc, IL, the heart of the *French Colonial Historic District* extending from nearby Kaskaskia to Cahokia, just south of East St. Louis. The restored Pierre Menard Home (c. 1800), includes a museum and slide show. North on *USH 3* is the restored *Fort de Chartres,* the center of French military and civic control until 1763. Staff and guides wear 18th century clothing. Museum and further information on French Louisiana is available here.

Grafton, Illinois
Population 918

There are numerous antique shops, stone buildings, and B&Bs in this picturesque river town which is located at the confluence of the Illinois/Mississippi rivers. A map with an historic walking tour of the town is available from local businesses.

RIVERLANDS INFORMATION CENTER (located on *STH 100,* 214 W. Main). This new visitor center provides information on the Illinois, Mississippi, and Missouri rivers.

THE SHAFER'S WHARF HISTORIC DISTRICT is located in the area of the Brown & Company building. During the late 1800s Shafer's Wharf was one of the largest commercial fish ports on the river. Fish were held live in large natural pens until purchased. They were then cleaned, salted, packed in barrels and shipped.

The stone pier built in 1874 can still be seen behind the Brown & Company building from the Great River Road. The stone saltbox building across the street was the warehouse.

The *Belle of Grafton* excursion boat is located at the boatyard where nationally known *Frieman Skiffs* were assembled between 1850 and 1920. The 17-acre boat yard is being developed into a yacht club and restaurant.

Grafton is situated along the shores of the 15-mile-long pool formed behind the Mel Price Lock & Dam (# 26). Also known as *Lake Alton,* the size of the pool makes it a favorite for recreational boating/yachting.

A Brief History of Grafton

Though founded in 1832 by James Mason, it is known that a block house at the confluence of the Illinois and the Mississippi rivers protected settlers as early as 1812. According to local historian, Mary Ann Pitchford, a ferry operated here in 1835 which helped cut in half the 40 mile river trip from Grafton to St. Louis.

Grafton's population peaked at 10,000 in the 1850s, due to employment offered at stone quarries, boat building, and commercial fishing industries. The local limestone was considered to be excellent building material and was used in constructing the historic *Eads Bridge* at St. Louis, the railroad bridge at Hannibal, MO, and the bridge in Quincy, IL. From 1866 to 1867 over 2,000 men worked the quarries.

The Mississippi River flows west to east from Grafton to Alton. Memorable sunsets emblazon the sky when driving or biking upriver from Alton to Grafton. The limestone bluffs, hill prairies, and broad Lake Alton make this one of the more scenic portions of the Great River Road.

Eagles perch in the bluffs and large winter concentrations can be seen soaring over the Great River Road and below Lock 26--as many as 200 have been counted in a single winter day!

SAM VADALABENE GREAT RIVER ROAD BIKE TRAIL. Bikers can also enjoy this scenic stretch of Great River Road and picturesque villages between Alton and Pere Marquette State Park. It is named for Illinois' ''Senator Sam'' who took a special interest in development of Illinois' Great River Road.

RAGING RIVERS WATER SLIDE PARK (just down river of Grafton). From the driveway of this resort community, the confluence of the Illinois and Mississippi rivers is visible to the

west, as is Calhoun Point. Since Kampsville, the opposite bank
has been Calhoun County, Illinois. Hereafter it will be the state
of Missouri.

PIASA CREEK (locally pronounced PIE-A-SAW) is said to mean
"one who devours men." See legend of the Piasa Bird page
215. Access to the Mississippi River · four concrete ramps ·
concession stand · day use · parking

NEW PIASA CHAUTAUQUA HISTORIC DISTRICT (Lo-
cated along *STH 100* between Elsah and Pere Marquette) is a
privately owned summer resort village. Art and drama classes
are still offered in the Chautauqua tradition.

*According to the Illinois Historic Preservation Agency,
Chautauqua was a 19th century social phenomenon that brought
culture to thousands of rural American locations. Chautauquas
took their name from Lake Chautauqua in New York where
summer camps that had originally been held to train Sunday
School teachers gradually expanded to include various forms of
popular entertainment such as lectures, concerts and even
fireworks.*

*In Illinois, Chautauqua tents sprang up at Galesburg,
Rock Island, and other sites. Chautauquas were usually held in
areas of natural beauty, especially near lakes and rivers where
the meetings assumed a holiday air.*

Elsah, Illinois
Population 125

Here is a traveler's treasure. This quaint river village,
circa 1850, is virtually unchanged due to its relative isolation
until the Great River Road came through in 1967. The *ENTIRE*

village is on the National Register of Historic Places. Look in the window of the restored Village Hall where simple Shaker-style chairs still hang from the wall on pegs. The Museum is open on weekends. The Parsonage beside the Methodist Church has presided over the same shaded corner since 1859.

Feel free to park and walk around. The entire settlement is only two streets wide and is replete with white stone cottages surrounded by color-bedecked floral gardens.

Expect fog shrouded, humid mornings that would be almost mystically silent but for an occasional car mumbling past the flowered window sills and gardens. Colorful maples, oak, and other bluffside hardwoods create an annual fall spectacle.

The tea room at the *Elsah Landing Cafe* is highly recommended for homemade breads, pastries, and pies. A general store, bakery, and three gift shops round out the commercial amenities of this little village. Three B&Bs: *The Green Tree Inn, Corner Nest,* and *Maple Leaf Cottages* offer lodging and breakfast in 19th century surroundings.

PRINCIPIA COLLEGE, the only Christian Science college in the world, is located at the top of the bluff just east of Elsah. The quiet, scenic locale, plus the fact that Elsah became a "dry" community after an alcohol related death in the 1930s, made it an attractive community for members of the Christian Science Church and for professors at Principia College.

Brief History of Elsah

Addison Green, Elsah's first settler, came in 1847 to chop wood for steamboats. His log cabin and river boat landing became known as *Jersey Landing.* The site is still easy to imagine. Immediately upon entering the town, the *Corner Nest* encapsulates Green's original log cabin. The low ground upon which the highway is built was the harbor for riverboats.

A Scotsman, James Semple, who was a general in the Black Hawk War, bought the valley from Grafton's James Mason in 1853. The name Elsah is believed to refer to *Ailsa Craig,* the last outcropping of cliffs his family saw when leaving Scotland. Semple offered free lots to anyone who built with stone from his quarry. As the mortar was made from Mississippi River sand, shells can still be seen in the mortar between the limestone blocks.

Elsah is nestled between two limestone bluffs in a narrow gorge-like valley that leads to the agricultural areas of Jersey County. The self-sufficient little settlement prospered as the main shipping point for Jersey County, as well as becoming a milling center for the area.

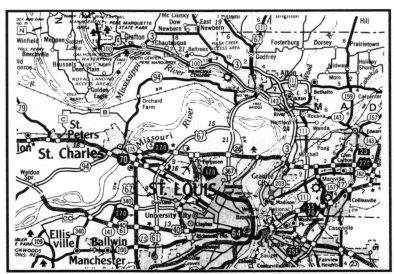

Grafton to Centerville, IL

"You'd have really liked it before 1965 when NOBODY drove through town," confides a woman on one of the town's many park benches. *"An old coon dog we called "Boomer" always slept in the middle of the street. Why, if a car DID drive through town, you'd have seen a face peeking out of every window."*

PORTAGE DES SIOUX, MO, is located on a narrow tongue of land, two miles wide, between the Mississippi and the Missouri rivers. Stilted homes are visible on the flat savanna and bottomland. It served as a portage for Indians and pioneers, which saved 25 miles over the river route to St. Louis.

OUR LADY OF THE WATERS is visible on the Missouri shore just east of Elsah. The illuminated shrine was built after Portage des Sioux was saved from the flood of 1951. The flood of 1973 crested over the top of its 17-foot high pedestal. During the annual spring *Blessing of the Fleet,* pleasure boaters motor from St. Louis to Portage des Sioux to have boats individually blessed.

PIASA BIRD (located along the Great River Road just north of Alton). Here is a billboard-like rendition of an Indian pictograph which was described by Marquette & Joliet in 1673 as a painting on the face of the limestone bluffs. The rocks bearing the actual drawing may have been quarried in 1856.

Marquette noted in his journal, *"We soon fell into the shadow of a tall promontory, and with great astonishment beheld the representations of two monsters painted on its lofty limestone front...It was an object of Indian worship, and greatly impressed me with the necessity of substituting for this monstrous idolatry the true God."*

The mythical creature, part man, part bird supposedly developed a taste for human flesh (particularly children) and terrorized a nearby Illini village until a chief noticed it had no protective scales on its underbelly. He offered himself as bait on the bluff-top and, as the creature swooped low to carry him off, hidden warriors were able to penetrate its vitals with arrows and spears, and the creature died.

Piasa Rock painting by Henry Lewis, Mississippi River Panorama Painter (1848).

MADISON COUNTY and GREATER ALTON

Alton, Illinois
Population 33,000

A major Con Agra flour mill along the Great River Road at the west end of town is reminiscent of the days when Alton's mills made it the fifth largest grain processor in the country. Today, flour continues to be milled and shipped nationwide, and Alton is in the center of a large industrial, chemical, steel, and oil refining area known as Greater Alton.

A Brief History of Alton

One hundred years after Pere Marquette recorded his observation of the Piasa Bird, Jean Baptiste Cardinal established a French outpost at the present site of Alton, IL. In 1803 *Meriwether Lewis* and *William Clark* camped at the point where the Wood River Creek emptied into the Mississippi at the confluence of the Missouri and Mississippi before beginning their epic expedition to the Pacific Ocean. In 1818 the city of Alton was platted by Col. Rufus Easton, the first postmaster of St. Louis. It was incorporated in 1837.

Its proximity to Missouri and the leadership of abolitionist Elijah Lovejoy made Alton a major terminal on the underground railroad. Several Alton homes still have underground tunnels and secret chambers where escaping slaves could be hidden. The better documented stations include the old stone house directly across from the College Avenue Presbyterian Church, where Elijah Lovejoy served as pastor, and the Enos House, a prominent 4-story stone Italianate located on Third Street.

The last of the Lincoln/Douglas debates was held at the corner of Market and Broadway in Alton. A marker commemorates the 1858 debate.

Places to Visit in Alton

HISTORIC DISTRICTS: Alton has several, including *Christian Hill Historic District* on State Street, *Middletown Historic District* on Henry Street, and the *Upper Alton Historic District* on College Avenue.

CONFEDERATE PRISON MONUMENT (200 William Street). This small portion of original stone wall from Illinois' first penitentiary was restored in 1973. The original prison was built in 1833 and closed in 1860 after after campaigns by prison reformer Dorothea Dix. It reopened in 1862 to house Confederate POWs. A second monument to 1,613 POWs who died of small pox is located at the historic cemetery on Rozier St.

SOUTHERN ILLINOIS UNIVERSITY DENTAL SCHOOL (2800 College Avenue) is housed in beautiful limestone buildings which were home to the *Schurtleff Girls College* from 1832 to 1957.

LOVEJOY MONUMENT (5th and Monument Avenue). Built in honor of Elijah Parish Lovejoy, editor of the Alton Telegraph and a pre-Civil War crusader for a free press and the abolition of slavery. Lovejoy was killed by a mob in 1837, his building burned, and his press thrown into the river. The yoke of his press was recovered 100 years later and is now on display at the offices of *The Telegraph,* 111 E. Broadway. A monument marks Lovejoy's grave at the Alton cemetery, 5th and Monument.

BELLE OF ALTON RIVERBOAT CASINO is located at the foot of Piasa Street. There is public parking and a free shuttle available from 7th and Piasa streets. No minors are allowed on board and there is no loss limit on Illinois riverboat casinos. For current information, call 1-800-336-SLOTS.

ALTON GIANT STATUE (commemorates Alton native, Robert Wadlow, the tallest man in history at 8' 11-1/2''). Life size bronze makes excellent photo opportunity for size comparisons. The Alton Museum of History and Art is located at 121 E. Broadway and contains Wadlow memorabilia.

ALTON ANTIQUE DISTRICT (bordering Broadway, between George and State Street). A 6-block area with over 40 antique shops located in 19th century buildings.

GORDON MOORE PARK (Off *STH 140).* Major city park of over 700 acres includes numerous sports fields, a lake, and the Nan Elliot Memorial Rose Garden with over 1,000 rose bushes. A new Arnold Palmer-designed golf course here joins eighteen other courses located in the three county area.

MELVIN PRICE LOCK & DAM #26 (off *STH 143* in Alton) is now in use, though construction continues on the Illinois side. With a price tag of over one billion dollars, it is the largest Army Corps of Engineers construction project in the nation. Tours of the old control room will be permitted once the new one is completed on the Illinois side.

The lock is long enough for a towboat and 15 barges to lock through in one piece. The lock became necessary because of the bottleneck of barges passing up the Illinois, the Mississippi, and the Missouri rivers. Before the new lock was opened in 1989, it was not unusual to have 20 to 30 tows backed up at the lock, requiring a wait of several days to "lock through."

U.S. ARMY CORPS OF ENGINEERS, St. Louis District. Demonstration unit for Environmental Engineering. A multimillion dollar visitor center will soon offer education exhibits and observation areas.

HARRIS PARK overlook (north on State Street, then follow Belleview to Riverview Park and overlook). Fine old homes along the bluff tops. Park provides dramatic overlook of the town, river, lock & dam, and Great River Road. On a clear day, the Gateway Arch in St. Louis is visible.

LEWIS AND CLARK STATE HISTORIC SITE (Just south of Hartford off *STH3*). Commemorates the point where Meriwether Lewis and William Clark spent the winter of 1783-84 before their expedition to the Pacific Ocean. The site also provides the best ground level view of the confluence of the Missouri and Mississippi rivers. Check road conditions as the area is quite low. Improvements, including the replica of an outpost fort, are being planned for adjacent higher ground. Picnicking · fishing · hiking

HORSESHOE LAKE STATE RECREATION AREA. 2,600-acre state park offers picnicking, boating, fishing, hunting, birding and camping. 18-hole golf course and water recreation center located nearby.

THE MISSOURI RIVER

This longest stream in the U.S. was named for the Missouri Indians. It begins at Three Forks, Montana, (elevation 4,032 feet) and flows 2,714 miles. Many considered it to be the main stream of the Mississippi River. The combined reach of the Missouri-Mississippi rivers is 3,741 miles, a length exceeded only by the Amazon and the Nile rivers. The Mississippi River, from source to mouth, is only 2,348 miles.

Granite City, Illinois
Population 32,862

LOCK & DAM 27. This last lock in the Upper Mississippi River Navigation Project is in the Chain of Rocks Canal at Granite City. The canal was built to bypass a rocky obstruction in the Mississippi River. The lock accommodates a full, 15 barge tow. From the first lock at the Falls of St. Anthony to the last, the river has dropped from an elevation of 680 feet to 384 feet over a distance of 699 miles.

South of this lock, the river is unimpeded by the lock & dam system. Travel on the river becomes notably more treacherous as the river runs faster, deeper, and becomes less stable. The rocky river bottom that is prevalent to the north, changes to a sandy, silty base that can run as deep as 5,000 feet in the Louisiana delta--the accumulated silt of eons. In fact, the boot shape of the Louisiana delta is nothing more than silt that has spilled over the edge of the mainland to fill in the continental shelf off the mouth of the Mississippi River.

Spanish explorers noted that the current of this river was so strong, the volume so great, that fresh water rather than salt water could be dipped a mile out into the Gulf of Mexico. Interestingly enough, the accumulated shells of tiny one-celled

Gulf organisms have provided compelling evidence of a vast flood of fresh water into the Gulf of Mexico about 11,600 years ago.

According to some scholars, catastrophic walls of ice broke from receding glaciers and joined the huge ice-melt runoff, scouring out the bluffland contours of the Mississippi River valley. It is envisioned that such a sudden collapse of the North American ice cap produced a massive sea-level rise that spread with the speed of a great tidal wave around the world in 24 hours. Perhaps it was this experience that produced a memory of the Biblical flood. The fossilized remains of the Gulf organisms show a marked decrease in salinity during a time correlating exactly with a clean, silty mud layer eight feet thick which archaeologists have found beneath vast expanses of Arabian desert.

> *Route to Cahokia Mounds follows STH 3 south to I-270 East to I-255 South (Exit 24) to Collinsville Road.*

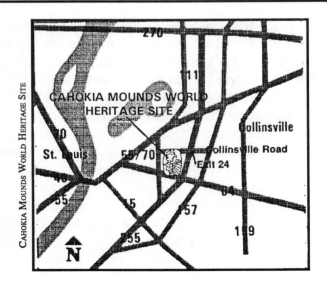

ST. CLAIRE COUNTY

General Arthur St. Clair, first governor of the Northwest Territories (northwest of the Ohio River), is the namesake of this first county in Illinois. It was established in 1790 though assuring law and order in this wilderness was no easy matter. In one case involving a $16 judgement, the Sheriff was required to serve a summons in Prairie du Chien, 400 miles to the north. He fitted out his canoe, including suitable stock for Indian trade, and delivered his papers as required. His mileage and expenses, added to the judgement, totaled $900.

CAHOKIA MOUNDS WORLD HERITAGE SITE (Collinsville, IL). One of the largest pre-Columbian archeological sites in the

MIKE COLES

View of the Cahokia Mounds World Heritage Site with Twin Mounds in the foreground and Monk's Mound at center back.

nation preserves the remains of the largest Indian city north of Mexico. When the 2,200 acre site was designated a *United Nations World Heritage Site* it joined an elite group of cultural landmarks considered to be of international significance in the history of mankind: the City of Rome, the Great Wall of China, the Pyramids of Egypt, and the Taj Mahal in India, the Grand Canyon, Yellowstone Park, and the Florida Everglades.

Visitors can tour an area of 65 earthen mounds, a wooden sun calendar, and enjoy an outstanding, newly completed interpretive center. Plan to spend several hours and be sure to see the 15 minute orientation slide show. A suggested self-guided tour is available for less than $1 at the gift shop.

It is estimated that over the course of 300 years, the Indians moved 50 million cubic feet of earth to build the mounds. The clay was dug with tools of wood, stone, or shell, and transported in baskets. Mounds were built in platform, conical, and ridgetop formations.

MONK'S MOUND (named for a group of French Monks who lived nearby from 1809-1813) is the largest prehistoric earthen construction in the New World--larger even than the Pyramids of Egypt. From its summit, the Gateway Arch and the city of St. Louis are visible. St. Louis, in fact, was nicknamed "Mound City" because of 26 mounds located in the downtown area before it was built.

Built in stages over a period of 300 years, Monk's Mound is 1,000 feet long, 700 feet wide, 140 feet high and covers an area of 14 acres. It would have taken 2,000 men two years to haul basketsful of clay to build the mound. A massive building 105' x 48' x 50' high stood on the highest platform. Here the principal ruler lived, conducted ceremonies, and governed the city below. 40 lesser mounds date from 1200 to 1500 A.D.

have been located on the site. Viewed from the center, the sunrise aligned with 22 different posts at different times of the year. Red cedar is still considered to be a sacred tree by many Indian groups.

It has been suggested that perhaps one reason for the decline of the Mississippian Culture was the environmental impact of depleting area supplies of cedar trees (actually a type of juniper). As land was deforested, increasing erosion would have ruined prime croplands and fishing spots, thus decreasing community health and wealth.

THE MISSISSIPPIAN CULTURE

Located on a broad, fertile flood plain, the site provided the Mississippian culture with rich soil, abundant plant and animal life, and access to an enormous trade network. The culture has been compared to the civilization in Egypt along the banks of the Nile.

The name *Cahokia is* taken from the group of Illini (or Illiniwek) Indians who maintained a small camp here at the time of the French Explorers. Like the Mesquakie (Fox) and Sac Indians, the Illini arrived in the area only shortly before the French explorers.

It is believed that the Cahokia site was first inhabited about 700 A.D. by prehistoric Indians of the Late Woodland Culture. They lived in small villages as hunters and gatherers, with small cultivated crops of corn.

Around 850-900 A.D. the Mississippian Culture emerged. Better technology (e.g., a stone hoe) made possible a rich, agricultural economy based on the cultivation of corn and squash. The prehistoric city of 20,000 to 40,000 Indians, supported a sophisticated political, social, and religious community.

According to the Illinois Preservation Agency, the Mississippians, like the Incas and Aztecs in Mexico, were sun worshippers. Four or five wooden sun calendars (called "Woodhenge" after the stone circles of England's "Stonehenge") were used to determine the seasons. Trade networks extended from the Gulf of Mexico to the Great Lakes, and from the Rocky Mountains to the Atlantic Ocean.

Satellite communities are known to have existed at the sites of modern-day towns of Mitchell, Dupo, Lebanon, East St. Louis, and St. Louis, not to mention several communities located as far north as southwestern Wisconsin and east to Kentucky.

The population of Cahokia began a gradual decline about 1300. By 1500 the city was abandoned. Whether as a result of climatic changes, social problems, depletion of natural resources, or disease, the reason for the decline remains unknown. Later tribes to inhabit the area had no oral traditions or knowledge which might link them to the Mississippians.

SPECIAL EVENTS

Calhoun County Apple Fest, July, Hardin. Live Entertainment

Old Settlers' Days, Kampsville. First week after Labor Day, Indian/Mountainmen Camp. Fiddlers contest. Old skills/crafts

The Hanging of the Greens, Elsah. Early December (even years only). Historic buildings decorated in Victorian styles are opened to the public. Period dress, music, food, drink, bazaar.

U.S. ARMY CORPS OF ENGINEERS

River sailing is popular on Lake Alton

Though the practice of "choking a stump" or tying riverboats to conveniently located trees is as old as steamboating itself, it has become an environmental issue in modern times. The practice literally does cause death to a tree as the bark is chewed away by the tie-line. In the photo above, note that after the tree in front-right died the line was attached to the next closest tree. The Army Corps of Engineers has begun installing mooring areas so that commercial towboats waiting to lock through do not have to tie barges to trees.

Appendix

WHERE TO LOOK FOR BIRDS
Pete Petersen, East Davenport Birder and Naturalist

One of the most interesting birds that winter in this portion of the Mississippi River is the Bald Eagle. Arriving about Thanksgiving time and remaining until early March, they are especially numerous around the lock and dams during extremely cold periods. The best vantage points include Lock 13, viewed from Illinois; Lock 14, viewed from either side; Lock 18, viewed from Illinois; and Lock 19, viewed from Iowa. The largest concentrations are below the locks as the eagles are searching out fish that have been injured going through the dams. Locks 13 and 19 have had over 200 eagles present at one time.

During the summer, look over the gulls at these locations for the less common species: the Glaucous, both dark-bodied species, the Mew, Western, and the California gull. A Slaty-backed gull has been seen at Lock 14 and Lock 26.

Rocky areas near the locks are good for Snow Buntings. Check the ducks for Old Squaw and the Scoters.

During spring migrations, ducks and geese can be found near Grafton, IL, and Wapello, IA, units of the Mark Twain National Wildlife Refuge. Lock 13 and nearby Spring Lake National Wildlife Refuge, on the Illinois side between Fulton and Savanna, are also very good for waterfowl in spring and fall.

Warblers and other forest birds migrate in good numbers throughout the Mississippi Valley. Especially productive are

Credit Island Park at Davenport, IA, Loud Thunder Forest Preserve near Andalusia, IL, and Crapo Park in Burlington, IA.

During the breeding season, Wildcat Den State Park near Muscatine, IA, can be counted on for Louisiana Waterthrush, Acadian Flycatcher, Northern Parula, and Kentucky Warbler. There is a good chance for Summer Tanager and Cerulean Warbler.

Those with a canoe will find the Prothonotary Warbler, Brown Creepers, and Pileated Woodpecker in all forested backwaters. Many heronery sites can be found, but care should be taken not to disturb the nesting birds. Breeding herons include the Great Blue, Black & Yellow Crowned Night Heron, Green-backed Heron, and Great Egret. Wood Ducks are very common backwater breeders and Hooded Mergansers can also be found. A large cormorant colony can be found about five miles above Lock 13, near the Iowa Shore.

Migrant shorebirds of over twenty species can be found on river mudflats in August. The water level is critical, but it is usually low at this season. The harbor at Credit Island Park in Davenport, IA, has produced American Avocet, Western, Sharp-tailed, and Buff-breasted Sandpipers, and Red-necked Phalarope. Many swallows follow the river in August and September, as well as Osprey and Caspian Terns.

In late September, the hawk migration can be dramatic when seen from bluff-top vantage points. Mississippi Palisades State Park along *STH 84,* just north of Savanna, IL, is a good spot, especially the first bluff-top spot to the south. As many as 2,800 Broad-winged Hawks have been seen here in one day!

November is a good time to check pine, spruce and hemlock groves for winter feeders such as Red and White-winged Crossbills, Evening Grosbeaks, and Pine Grosbeaks. A good spot is Fairmont Cemetery in the western part of Davenport, IA.

Appendix B
Brief History of the Middle Mississippi River Valley

Under the Spanish Flag

1541	DeSoto is first European to explore southern reaches of the Missississippi.
1764	While Spain controls Missouri, few immigrants are Spanish. Daniel Boone arrives in 1798 to a grant of 8,500 acres. Others from Kentucky and Tennesee are recruited.
1790	Julien Dubuque acquires the Spanish Lead Mines in Iowa.

Under the French Flag

1673	Marquette and Jolliet record their travels on the Mississippi River south to Arkansas, then up the Illinois River.
1720	The French control the fur trade and governors of the Upper Mississippi River valley.
1735	Ste. Genevieve is first enduring colony in French Missouri.
1764	St. Louis founded by Pierre LeClede and his young stepson, Auguste Chouteau. Settled by uneasy Frenchmen recruited from Kaskaskia, Cahokia, and Fort de Chartres when Illinois was ceded by the French to the English. Unbeknownst to the settlers, the west bank had been ceded to Spain by France this same year.

Under the American Flag

1783	America wins independence from England.
1787	U.S. Government forbids slavery north of the Ohio River
1803	Napoleon offers President Thomas Jefferson the vast reaches along the Mississippi and Missouri rivers for $15 million.
1804	The Lewis and Clark Expedition strengthens U.S. claims from St. Louis to the Pacific. Meriwether Lewis and William Clark are led through the Rocky Mountains by Indian woman, Sacajawea. Lt. Zebulon Pike surveys the Upper Mississippi River valley to establish sites for government forts. In a fraudulently obtained treaty, the Sac/Mesquakie Indians relinquish all rights to land along the Rock River.
1811-12	Earthquake at New Madrid, MO (pronounced MAD-rid). Black Hawk and the Sac Indians side with the British in the *War of 1812.*
1816	Land grants in the *Illinois Military Tract* awarded to veterans of War of 1812.
1817	The first steamboat, *Zebulon Pike,* puffs from Louisville to

St. Louis. In 1823 *Virginia* steams all the way to Fort Snelling. By the 1850s St. Louis received more than 3,000 steamboats and a million tons of freight per year. In 1989, barges carrying more than 8 million tons passed through the Alton Dam just to the north of St. Louis.

1818   Illinois becomes 21st state. Land grants increase friction between settlers and native Indians.

1820   The Missouri Compromise allows Missouri admittance to the Union as a slave state, though the boundary line would henceforth be the southern boundary of Missouri. This was allowed to counterbalance Maine which became a free state at the same time.

1821   President James Monroe names Missouri as the 24th state. Stephen Austin leaves with 300 Missourians to settle his Texas land grant.

1822   Missourian William Becknell forges the trail to Santa Fe, returning with silver bullion and *mules*. Lead mining leases are let in the Wisconsin Territory.

1828   Kit Carson leaves Missouri for the Santa Fe trail.

1829   Northwestern Illinois is opened for white settlement and Sac/Mesquakie agree to move to western bank of the Mississippi River.

1831   Joseph Smith and his Saints (Mormons) begin flooding into the Independence area. Here begins fifty years of internal torment. Mormons are brutally driven from the state in 1839. Then bloody conflicts consume the western part of the state over the future of slavery between Kansas and Missouri. Bitter vengance became standard through the Civil War. This was followed by a period of lawlessness which finally culminated in the death of Jesse James in the 1880s. (from *Missouri, A History* by Paul C. Nagel)

1832   Black Hawk War ends in bloody defeat for Sac nation. Black Hawk Purchase opens Iowa to white settlement.

1839   Mormons flee to Quincy, IL, establish Nauvoo.

1846   Iowa named 29th state in the Union.

1849   The song "Sweet Betsy from Pike (County)" immortalizes thousands who left for the Oregon Trail and the California Gold Rush via Missouri and Iowa. Even larger numbers of Mormons followed Brigham Young along the Mormon Trail to the Great Salt Lake Basin.

1858   Lincoln-Douglas debates

1861	Invention of the telegraph puts an end to the year-long saga of the Pony Express out of St. Joseph, MO. Brigham Young sends the first telegram: *Utah stands firm with the Union.*
1861	Civil War. More than 1,000 battles and skirmishes were fought in Missouri; more than in any state but Virginia and Tennessee.
1874	Eads Bridge (the "impossible" bridge) spans the Mississippi River at St. Louis. Engineer James Eads (American Hall of Fame) also built the ironclad boats that permitted Federal boats to claim the Mississippi River during Civil War.
1904	World's Fair held in St. Louis commemorates 100 year centenial of Lewis & Clark Expedition.
1927	Charles Lindburgh flies the *Spirit of St. Louis* from New York to Paris.

Appendix C
A Guide to Mississippi River Miles--Dubuque to St. Louis

While river miles are not a major concern to the road traveler, they become very important to the river traveler who will find that even well-known towns and villages look quite different when seen from the water.

River miles for the Upper river are counted from 0 at Cairo (KAY-ro), IL, to Mile 839 at Lambert Landing in St. Paul, MN. River miles for the Lower Mississippi begin at 0 at Head of Passes, 90 miles below New Orleans, LA, and increase to Mile 953 at Cairo. A listing of river miles for major landmarks and towns along the river follows.

583	Lock & Dam 11. 581.7 WI/IL state line.
580	Dubuque, IA
565	Galena R. enters the Mississippi R. City of Galena, IL, 4 miles inland.
556.7	Bellevue, IA, and Lock & Dam 12.
545.2	Army Ordinance testing ground (IL shore) is closed to public through mile 548.5

537	Savanna, IL. 539 Mississippi Palisades State Park.
535	Sabula, IA. 533 to 522 is a wide stretch. 6' to 10' waves possible.
522.5	Clinton, IA. Lock & Dam 13. 519 Fulton, IL.
511.7	Comanche, IA.
502.5	Cordova, IL. Quad Cities Nuclear Power Plant.
502	Princeton, IA.
493.1	LeClaire, IA. Lock & Dam 14.
495	Bettendorf, IA.
483	Davenport, IA.
482.9	Rock Island, IL. Lock & Dam 15 (double lock).
457.1	Muscatine, IA. Lock & Dam 16.
437.1	New Boston, IL. Lock & Dam 17.
416	Oquawka, IL. 418 Delabar State Park.
410.5	Lock & Dam 18.
404	Burlington, IA.
383	Fort Madison, IA.
373.6	Nauvoo, IL.
365.2	Keokuk, IA. Lock & Dam 19. (Only dam besides #1 to produce electricity. 56 mile pool is called Lake Cooper or Keokuk Lake.)
364	Hamilton, IL. Largest producers of beekeeper supplies.
361	Des Moines River mouth.
342.2	Canton, MO. Lock & Dam 20.
324.9	Quincy, IL. Lock & Dam 21.
308	Hannibal, MO. 301 Lock & Dam 22 at Saverton, MO. THERE IS NO LOCK 23.
273.4	Clarksville, MO. Lock & Dam 24.
241.4	Winfield, MO. Lock & Dam 25.
209.4	Piasa Creek enters Mississippi R.
202.9	Alton, IL. Lock & Dam 26 built 2 miles below old lock.
185	Granite City, IL. 184-195 Lock 27.
195.4	Missouri River mouth. St. Charles, MO, has newly restored riverfront (Frenchtown).
179.5	St. Louis, MO. Historic LeClede levee. Jefferson National Expansion Memorial riverfront park. 630' high Gateway Arch. Lewis & Clark Museum. Old Cathedral. Old Court house. Railroad cars were ferried across the river from East St. Louis until construction of Eads Bridge.

Appendix D

Do you need information on lodging, attractions, or local events? Listed here are many organizations which are more than happy to help.

STATE Departments of Tourism

Iowa: Travel & Tourism Division, 600 E. Court St., Des Moines, IA 50309. Call 800-345-IOWA or FAX 515-281-7276

Illinois: Bureau of Tourism, 620 E. Adams, Springfield, IL 62701. Call 217-785-6352 or 800-223-0121. FAX 217-785-6454

Missouri: Missouri Division of Tourism, Truman State Office Bldg., PO Box 1055, Jefferson City, Missouri 65102.

REGIONAL Tourism Agencies

Eastern Iowa Tourism Assoc.
PO Box 178, S. Downey St.
West Branch, IA 52358
319-643-2848
800-348-1837

Mississippi River Parkway Commission
Suite 1513, 336 Robert St.
St. Paul, MN 55101
612-224-9903 or
FAX 612-297-6896

Galena/Jo Daviess County CVB
101 Bouthillier St.
Galena, IL 61036
800-747-9377

Rock Island District,
U.S. Army Corps of Engineers
Mississippi River Visitor Center, Clock Tower Bldg.
PO Box 2004
Rock Island, IL 61204-2004
309-788-6361, ext. 338

Mississippi Valley Welcome Center
900 Eagle Ridge Road
Le Claire, IA 52753
319-289-3009
800-933-0708

IOWA Contacts

Bellevue Chamber
Bellevue, IA 52031
319-872-4991

Bettendorf Tourism Bureau
1708 Grant St.
Bettendorf, IA 52722
319-355-4753

Burlington CVB
807 Jefferson
Burlington, IA
319-752-7009

Clinton CVB
333 4th Ave. So, PO Box 527
Clinton, IA 52732
319-242-5702

Davenport Area CVB
108 East Third St.
Davenport, IA 52801
319-322-5142
800-747-7025

Dubuque CVB
800-79-VISIT

Fort Madison Chamber
933 Avenue H, Box 277
Fort Madison, IA 52627
319-372-5471
800-369-FORT

Jackson County EDC
201 West Platt Street
Maquoketa, IA 52060
800-342-1837 or 319-687-2237

Keokuk Area CTB
401 Main St.
Keokuk, IA 52632
319-524-5055

Muscatine CVB
319 E. Second St.
P.O. Box 297
Muscatine, IA 52761
319-263-8895

St. Donatus Information
P.O. Box 74
St. Donatus, IA 52071
319-773-2405

ILLINOIS Contacts

Alton/Twin Rivers Area CVB
200 Piasa St
Alton, IL 62002
618-465-6676 or
800-258-6645

Bed & Breakfast Guide
Illinois B&B Association
PO Box 96, 15 Mill
Elsah, IL 62028

Bishop Hill Arts Council
PO Box 47
Bishop Hill, IL 61419
309-927-3345

Collinsville CVB
One Gateway Drive
Collinsville, IL 62234
618-345-4999

Elsah Information
PO Box 96
Elsah, IL 62028
618-374-2821

Fort de Chartres
Prairie du Rocher, IL 62277
618-284-7230

Galena/Jo Daviess CVB
Galena, IL 61036
800-747-9377

Uptown Nauvoo Tourism
Box 41
Nauvoo, IL 62354
217-453-6648

LDS Nauvoo Visitor Center
PO Box 215
Nauvoo, IL 62354
217-453-2237

Quad City Visitors Bureau, 329
18th St.
Rock Island, IL 61202
309-788-7800 or
800-474-7800

Quincy CVB
WCU Building, 510 Main St.
Quincy, IL 62301
217-223-1000
800-458-4552

Savanna Chamber
PO Box 315
Savanna, IL 61074
815-273-2722

Warsaw Information Center
Warsaw, IL 62379
217-256-4235

Whiteside County Tourism
Thomson, IL 61285
815-259-5665

Yellow Banks Territory
RR 2, Box 225
Aledo, IL 61231
309-582-7551

MISSOURI Contacts

Great River Road Interpretive
Center, 66 S. Main St.
Ste. Genevieve, MO 63670
314-883-7097

St. Charles CVC
230 South Main St,, PO Box 300
St. Charles, MO 63102
314-421-1023
800-247-9791

Missouri B&B Association
PO Box 31246
St. Louis, MO 63131
314-965-4328

Jefferson National Expansion
Memorial, 11 N. 4th St.
St. Louis, MO 63102
314-425-4465

Hannibal CVB
320 Broadway, PO Box 624
Hannibal, MO 63401
314-221-2477

St. Louis, MO, TVC
800-247-9791

Index

Index

"I have looked upon the Mississippi since I was a child. I love the great river...Mine was a beautiful country. I liked my towns, my cornfields, and the home of my people. I fought for them; it is now yours. Keep it as we did. It will produce you good crops."

from Black Hawk's farewell speech,
4th of July, 1838

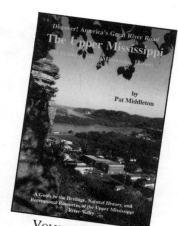